# WHAT IS *RIBA* ?

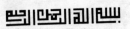

# WHAT
# IS
# RIBA
# ?

IQBAL AHMAD KHAN
SUHAIL

*Edited by*
Zafarul-Islam Khan, PhD

PHAROS

This is a translation of
*'Allamah* Iqbal Ahmad Khan Suhail's
*Haqiqatu'r-riba* حقيقة الربا,
first published in Urdu at Aligarh in 1936.
This translation follows
the new edited Urdu version.
An Arabic translation
as well as the new Urdu edition
are available from the publishers of this book.

*Translation from Urdu*
Rizwanullah & Zafarul-Islam Khan

*Help in authentication of Arabic texts*
'Abdul Hafiz M Yunus & 'Abdullah 'Abdur Rahman

*Translation of Persian texts*
Muhammad Ilyas

First English edition 1999

© Pharos Media & Publishing Pvt Ltd, 1999.

**PUBLISHERS**
Pharos Media & Publishing Pvt Ltd
P.O.Box 9701, D-84 Abul Fazl Enclave-I
Jamia Nagar, New Delhi 110 025 India
*Fax*: (+9111) 683 5825
*E-mail*: zik@vsnl.com
          zik.pharos@aworld.net
*Internet:* www.pharosmedia.com

ISBN  81 - 7221 - 013 - 2

*PRINTED IN INDIA*

# TABLE OF CONTENTS

Introduction    *Dr Maqbool Ahmad*    9

Foreword to the first edition    *Sayyid Tufail Ahmad*    13

Various commercial dealings (chart)    18

1.  Dichotomy of belief and practice
    regarding 'interest'    19

2.  Disadvantages of the wrong definition
    of *sood*/interest    21

3.  Studying the issue of *riba*    26

4.  Rational definitions of 'interest' and *riba*    28

5.  'Interest' and *riba* are not synonymous    29

6.  No consensus about the definition of *riba*    30

7.  Definition of *riba* by Hanafi *Fuqaha*    33

8.  *Kayl* and *bay$^c$* explained    34

9.  Increment of commodity is not *riba*    35

10. Some principles about the reliability of *hadiths*    46

11. Kinds of Narrations and their examples    50

    a.  The first narration    52

    b.  The second narration    54

    c.  Some instructions of the Holy Prophet (*pbuh*)
        about the conquest of Khaybar which have been
        wrongly used in the arguments regarding *riba*    57

    d.  The third narration    59

    e.  The fourth narration    60

    f.  $^c$Ubaydullah's Narration    63

12. Instructions about *muratalah* and *bay$^c$ sarf*
    mixed up with *riba*    69

13. Instructions about mutual exchange of coins
    have no connection with *riba*    70

14. Instructions of the Prophet about *bay$^c$ sarf*    72

15. Some narrations about *bay$^c$ sarf*    73

    a.  Abu Sa$^c$id al-Khudari's narrative    73

    b.  Abu Hurayrah's narrative    75

16. A review of the *ahadith* regarding *riba al-nasi'ah*
    (credit usury)    81

17. Mistakes of the first inference    86

5

| | | |
|---|---|---|
| 18. | Details of the second inference | 87 |
| 19. | Reasons for *riba* in storable edibles | 89 |
| 20. | Prevalent practices of interest | 93 |
| 21. | *Riba* practices in early Arabia: *bayᶜ salaf* and *riba* | 94 |
| 22. | *Imam* al-Baghawi's interpretation of the *riba* verse | 97 |
| 23. | Irrationality of the definition of *riba* by *fuqaha* | 98 |
| 24. | Rules must vary in accordance with differences in deals, persons and situations | 99 |
| | *(a)* Purpose of the deal | 99 |
| | *(b)* Parties to the deal | 100 |
| | *(c)* Location of the deal | 100 |
| 25. | Details of objections on 'b' and 'c' | 101 |
| 26. | Sayings of *sahaba* and inferences of *fuqaha* are mixed up with *ahadith* of the Prophet | 102 |
| 27. | Narrations regarding *riba* | 104 |
| 28. | No *riba* between a *harbi* and a Muslim | 104 |
| 29. | The difference between the Prophet's *(pbuh)* increase and the *bayᶜ salaf* of al-ᶜAbbas | 107 |
| 30. | Conditions where increase is permissible and where it is not | 111 |
| | *a.* Zakat and *riba* compared | 111 |
| | *b.* Result of Jews' disobedience | 112 |
| | *c.* 'Eating property wrongfully' | 113 |
| | *d.* Meaning of 'trade' | 113 |
| | *e.* Criterion of mutual consent | 114 |
| 31. | Which *riba* was forbidden to the Jews | 117 |
| 32. | Verses of the *Bible* regarding *riba* | 117 |
| 33. | Two *rukuᶜs* on the prohibition of *riba* | 119 |
| 34. | The Third *rukuᶜ* prohibiting *riba* | 122 |
| 35. | The time of the third *rukuᶜ* and the cause of its revelation | 123 |
| 36. | Some narrations about the cause of the verse's revelation | 125 |
| 37. | Conclusions of the foregoing discussion and their non-applicability in India | 127 |
| 38. | The course of action in the absence of a clear definition of *riba* | 128 |

6

|  |  |  |
|---|---|---|
| | *a.* Tradition of the Arabs | 129 |
| | *b.* Inference (*qiyas*) and its details | 129 |
| 39. | Advance purchase of crops by al-ᶜAbbas | 130 |
| 40. | Inference of some ᶜ*ulama* from the order regarding advance purchase | 131 |
| 41. | Rational reasons for my disagreement with the said inference by ᶜ*ulama* | 132 |
| 42. | The inference of the author | 140 |
| 43. | Reasons for my inference in the light of Islamic sources | 141 |
| 44. | Our claim supported by the verse proscribing *riba* | 142 |
| 45. | Studying the verse forbidding *riba* | 143 |
| 46. | Similarity between loans and *bay*ᶜ | 144 |
| 47. | *Riba* and *sadaqah* compared | 146 |
| 48. | Three methods of meeting needs | 147 |
| 49. | Obligation of *qard hasan* | 148 |
| 50. | Explanation of the verse 2:279 | 148 |
| 51. | Need is a necessary condition for *riba* | 151 |
| 52. | Revelation of the verse for relinquishing *riba* | 152 |
| 53. | Our inference about *riba* | 153 |
| 54. | Jews and Muslims have the same *riba* | 154 |
| 55. | The reason for restricting the application of the rule of *riba* to *Dar al-Islam* | 156 |
| | *a.* Community's benefit through individual help | 156 |
| | *b.* The Connection of *riba* with business | 159 |
| 56. | Mak-hul's narration is correct according to rationality and justice | 160 |
| | Anecdote 1 | 161 |
| | Anecdote 2 | 164 |
| 57. | Definition of *Dar al-harb* and *harbi* | 166 |
| | *Appendix 1: Fatwa* on bank interest & insurance | 173 |
| | *Appendix 2:* Rethinking the '*riba*' issue | 193 |
| | List of sources used to authenticate the Arabic texts in the book | 196 |
| | Glossary | 197 |

# INTRODUCTION

*In the name of Allah,*
*the Most Merciful, the Most Gracious*

All praise to Allah, the Sustainer of the worlds, and prayers and greetings to the Last of the Prophets.

It is a great tragedy of the Muslim *Ummah* that the powerful and stable *Khilafat-e Rashidah* did not last for long. As a result many tasks were left incomplete and remain so until this day.

The Qur'an, written on many materials, was in the safe custody of a number of people in the early days of Islam. During the period of the third caliph, 'Uthman ibn 'Affan, all these fragmented portions were compiled in one single master copy under the supervision of the Prophet's companions who had memorized the whole Qur'an. Copies of this master copy were sent to all parts of the lands of Islam. Therefore, every copy of the Qur'an found anywhere in the world today is exactly like the original one. There is no possibility of variance or difference on this count among Muslims.

The same was supposed to be the case with the *Hadith*, the sayings and deeds of the Prophet. Next would have been the turn of early Islamic history. But after the fall of the *Khilafat-e Rashidah*, the system of *Imamah* and governance became children's playground. Lack of stability did not permit the completion of the fundamental task of compiling an official and certified collection of the reliable *hadiths* after destroying all the weak and fabricated ones. This would have closed many a door leading to dissension and disunity in the *Ummah*.

9

The same should have been done with early Islamic history. Early historians had collected a lot of raw material. A team of experts should have examined all this matter and compiled the reliable narratives and destroyed the rest of the baseless lot. This task was also left unfinished.

There is no doubt that individual scholars and *imams* have done great service in these fields in their individual capacity. But, being individual and private endeavours bereft of the caliphal endorsement, these efforts did not gain general acceptance.

For many centuries the *Ummah* is suffering due to disputes emanating from this short-coming. It would be a great service to Islam if Muslim states even today selected expert scholars from all over the World of Islam and entrusted them with this task with due means. If this could happen, a few years' concerted and serious effort will lead to the compilation of reliable collections of *Hadith* and Islamic history.

A similar situation exists in respect of *fiqhi* issues also. There are some issues about which there is no difference of opinion but they have been neglected totally on the practical field. For instance, the share due to women in the property of their parents. In the presence of clear Qur'anic injunctions there is no scope for difference here. In fact, no difference of opinion does exist on this issue. But, as far as the Muslims of the Subcontinent are concerned, with a few exceptions here and there, there is a consensus to deprive their sisters and daughters of their due share in the *mirath*, inheritance, with nothing disturbing their conscience.

*Sunnah*, the Prophet's prescribed way about divorce has been totally neglected. There is no effort to follow the Qur'anic injunction in the event of differences between husband and wife, that is to try to solve the issue by each side appointing a mediator, *hakam*, who would try to find an amicable solution. The seriousness that the issue of divorce commands and the legal ways to go about it are both neglected. And in the event of divorce, there is no regard to the rights of the wife and the clear injunctions to treat her decently even after the pronunciation of divorce are mostly observed in violation.

There are certain problems which were never accorded the seriousness they deserved or have attained in the changed circumstances. For instance, the issue of Zakat. There is Zakat on agricultural produce even if a farmer produces only a few tons of wheat or the like. But there is no Zakat (in view of the Hanafis) on a salaried person who earns millions in a year and spends it all. (*Allamah* Yusuf al-Qaradawi and others have said that a salaried person must pay 2.5 percent of his annual salary). This issue has not been properly studied after the currency of the system of salaries as a means of income.

Likewise there are the problems of insurance and 'usury' (*sood/riba*). Some scholars have declared them legal and permissible in view of the special conditions prevailing in India but some others are still adamant about their illegality.

*Sood* (usury) has been described in the Qur'an as *riba* but it has not been explained and categorically defined. There are some indications in the *Hadith*. *Fuqaha* have dealt with *riba* relatively extensively but even they have differences of opinion.

Today the whole world is in the grip of Jewish and western capitalists who have introduced *riba* in every form of contemporary business. It is a serious task to find ways and solutions to protect ourselves from their tentacles and to ensure, at the same time, that the Muslim *Ummah* is not left out in the cold in the economic sphere.

A crucial issue in this respect is inflation. Earlier when we had gold and silver coins, their purchase value remained static for centuries. But today, as in India, the paper currency loses its value constantly and every year sees a fall in its purchasing power. Whatever was available for one hundred *rupees* a year ago will be available for a higher price a year later. This trend is continuing without any sign of change.

11

The then Grand *Mufti* of Darul ᶜUlum (Waqf), Deoband, *Mawlana* Sayyid Ahmad ᶜAli Saᶜid, may Allah have mercy upon him, had expressed his opinion in detail on this issue (*see appendix*). He explained that in India and similar countries, which do not fall within *Dar al-Islam*, interest paid by banks is permissible. Likewise insurance is also allowed. The *Mufti* of Darul ᶜUlum, Deoband, *Mawlana* Muhammad Zafeeruddin, has expressed similar opinion. But there are scholars who still differ on this point.

ᶜ*Allamah* Iqbal Ahmad Khan Suhail, who was a very learned scholar in Islamic sciences, published a treatise on *riba* about half a century ago . In it he studied the issue in great detail, defined *riba* and its various categories, discussed the narratives about it and evaluated the various opinions about their permissibility or otherwise. This book was not available for many years. Now it is being reprinted for the consideration of scholars and the elite of the *Ummah* so that they may reach a studied consensus after discussions. This issue is of utmost importance to the economy of the *Ummah*. *Riba*, on the other hand, has been denounced in the Qur'an in a way which no believer can overlook. It is, therefore, the need of the time that a consensus opinion should emerge on this crucial issue for the general Muslim public to follow.

*O Allah, show us truth as truth and bestow upon us its following and show us untruth as untruth and grant us its avoidance.*

Calcutta,                                              *Dr Maqbool Ahmad*
1 December 1998

# FOREWORD
## to the first edition

### Sayyid Tufail Ahmad
(author, *Muslamanon ka roshan mustaqbil*)

A number of books have appeared in Urdu on the issue of interest/usury but none is as comprehensive as this work, *Haqiqatur-riba*. Its author is *Mawlana* Iqbal Ahmad Suhail of Azamgarh. His greatest characteristic is that he mastered religious learning and then completed modern education. It may be said, therefore, that he is best qualified to study religious issues in the light of worldly needs and modern knowledge. At the age of 13 he became a disciple of *Mawlana* Shibli Nu'mani in 1899 and in 1908 started studying under *Mawlana* Shibli's able cousin, *Mawlana* Hamiduddin [Farahi] and completed the Arabic curriculum. In 1918 he completed his MA and LLB from Aligarh Muslim University.

*Mawlana* Suhail has penned his thoughts in this treatise at the instance of *Mawlawi* 'Abdul Ghani Ansari, BA, assistant commissioner, Income Tax, U.P., so that other people also may benefit from them.

*Mawlana* Suhail has explained the reality of *riba* in his words as follows:

Literally, *riba* ربا means an absolute raise or increase. But it is absolutely certain that any raise or increase, or *riba*, is not *'the riba'* prohibited by the *Shari'ah*. Thus all the verses of the Holy Qur'an regarding the prohibition of *riba* mention it as *'al-riba'* [*the riba*], that is, with the definite article *'al-'*. Certainly the definite article, *'al-'*, here is not indefinite or general, otherwise every form of monetary increase, such as business profit, would have been prohibited. So the *'al-'* here is specific and some special kind of increase has been prohibited under the *Shari'ah*. Let us see what is that special kind. In the Holy Qur'an itself neither is there any explicit description of that special

13

sort nor is there any explicit definition of the word *riba*. So we must refer to *ahadith* to see if the Holy Prophet (*pbuh*) has defined it in any way. But the Prophet also did not explicitly define *riba*.

The above quotation shows, at least, that *every 'riba'* is not *'the riba'* which is *haram* (unlawful). Otherwise *ᶜulama* could not dare to allow certain kinds of *riba* — for instance *riba* in *Dar al-harb* is not *haram*.

Now which *riba* is *haram*? *Mawlana* Suhail has explained that there is no definition of *riba* in the Qur'an and has quoted a saying of ᶜUmar ibn al-Khattab, may Allah be pleased with him, that :

إن آخر ما نزل من القرآن آية الربا وإن رسول الله صلـى الله عليـه وسـلم
قبض و لم يفسرها فدعوا الربا والرية (مسند أحمد، مسند عمـر بن الخطاب ، الحديـث
٢٤٨ ، ج ١،ص ٦٠) .

The Qur'anic *ayah* regarding *riba* is the last part of the Qur'an revealed, and the Holy Prophet (*pbuh*) died before interpreting this *ayah*. So give up *riba* and anything that you doubt.

Due to these circumstances the definition of *riba* rests solely on the *qiyas* (inference) of the *fuqaha*. But it is clear from the *fuqaha*'s views that there is a lot of difference among them, which has been studied by *Mawlana* Suhail in a section of this treatise. It has been shown that *fuqaha* have normally mixed up *riba* with *muratalah* and *sarf*, although these two types of commercial transactions have nothing to do with *riba*.

*Muratalah*, or 'barter' in English, means exchange in kind of various goods. Likewise *sarf*, or 'exchange' in English, means exchange of one coin or currency with another. Since coins were not common in old days, whenever one wanted to buy something he took something from his home, like grains or whatever was sought after in the markets, and exchanged it with something else like shoes or clothes and other necessities. Sometimes it involved exchange of various varieties of the same kind. Therefore, there were many rules about such transactions.

Likewise, in early Islam many coins from various countries, unequal in weight and value, used to be found in markets. There were problems about their sale and

14

purchase. *Mawlana* Suhail has shown that these too have nothing to do with *riba*. *Fuqaha* have considered the two aforementioned kinds of transactions as '*riba al-fadl*,' that is, an increase by one party while exchanging kind-with-kind, by way of weight, measure or number. But today barter is rare in civilized societies. Moreover, unequal coins, in shape or weight, are not found today. Therefore, *muratalah* and *sarf* transactions are outside the purview of our study. These two kinds of transactions are called '*riba al-fadl*' by *fuqaha*. But in fact these are not '*riba*' and the Prophet, upon whom be peace, did not consider them as *riba*.

Now only one kind of trading is left which is called *bay$^c$ salaf*, which means advance sale or credit surcharge on sale of goods. In other words, to buy something and pay for it but allowing a grace period for the delivery of the goods bought. Within this also fall loans taken for a certain period. In both these dealings if the person, who has sold something in advance or has taken a loan, fails to deliver at the appointed time, he agrees to an increase in the price or loan in order to gain another grace period. In *fiqh* this addition is called *riba al-nasi'ah* ربا النسينة , *i.e.*, price escalation in the case of advance or credit dealings. A discussion is possible only about *this* kind of dealings, since there is a *hadith* about *riba al-fadl* which says that لا ربا فيما كان يـدا بيـد (there is no *riba* in hand-to-hand dealings). Moreover, there is a clear *hadith* which says: لا ربا إلا فى النسينة (there is no *riba* except in advance or credit dealings). With these clear textual evidences the whole edifice of *riba*, except in credit dealings is demolished.

Now about credit dealings: every such dealing may be described as '*riba*' in the literal sense since it involves a value addition. But in view of *fiqh* not every addition or increase is the unlawful '*riba*'. This is why the *Mawlana* has studied the trade dealings prevalent in pre-Islamic Arabia and compared them with the dealings common today.

In ancient Arabia, a common method of credit dealing was for a person to take, for instance, one *maund*[1] of grain from a person against a promise to pay back one *maund* or

---

[1]   *Maund* [Hindi: *mun* – pronounced as 'shun'] is an Indian weight equal to around 82 pounds/37 kgs (ed.).

one and a half *maund* at the time of the next harvest. It was not agreed at the time of the deal how much more would the debtor pay if he failed to pay up at the appointed time. Now when he was unable to pay back in part or full, the creditor had the right to increase at will whatever quantity he liked against advancing the payment period. This is the type of dealing which is prohibited since the debtor is totally helpless *vis-à-vis* the creditor. Contrary to this, in modern times it is agreed *in advance* how much more the debtor will pay should he fail to repay on time. This is why present-day transactions cannot fall under the same category of transactions which were common in pre-Islamic Arabia.

The *riba* of ancient Arabia made *haram* is the '*riba* of Al-ᶜAbbas' [the Prophet's uncle], about which the Prophet declared in his sermon at the Last Pilgrimage: 'the first *riba* abolished is the *riba* of al-ᶜAbbas.' And this is the *riba* in which it is not agreed at the time of the dealing how much more the debtor will pay if he failed to repay within the appointed time.

The other characteristic of the ancient Arabian *riba*, as described by *Mawlana* Suhail, is that it was extracted from the poor and needy. To prove this, the author has quoted at length Qur'anic verses which have abolished the *riba*. The characteristic of these verses is that *riba* is compared with *Zakat* and *sadaqat* and the virtues of *Zakat* and *sadaqat* are enumerated *vis-à-vis riba* whose evils are described. This means that the people who paid *riba* were eligible to take *Zakat* and *sadaqat* and, therefore, taking *riba* from them was pronounced unlawful.

Likewise, the author has quoted a few verses from the *Bible* which show that the *riba* made unlawful for Jews took the shape of an additional amount of money charged for giving loans to needy brothers-in-faith in their own country. This same *riba* is unlawful for Muslims too, *i.e.*, the *riba* taken from a poor brother-in-faith who is eligible to take *Zakat* and *sadaqat*, in *Dar al-Islam*, where Muslims rule and where Islamic laws are enforced, against a loan given to alleviate a basic and real need. In this context the *Mawlana* has shown that the same rule applied in *Dar al-Islam* to the Muslim and the *dhimmi*. Just as taking *riba* from a needy Muslim is unlawful in *Dar al-Islam,* so is taking it from a poor *dhimmi* there.

The following is the summary of the rules of *riba* in the words of *Mawlana* Suhail:

> If a poor person who is entitled to take *sadaqat* [charity], takes a loan to sustain himself or his family; or a debtor who is unable to pay his dues and in the case of paying back his dues he will not be left with enough money to maintain his family, enters into an agreement for an increase over the amount due or on the actual loan then this is an agreement of *riba* which is unlawful. But this non-permissibility is conditional on two factors:
>
> (*a*) the place where this agreement is made should be under Islamic rule, that is where the government's orders are issued according to the intent of the *Shari'ah* even in financial matters.
>
> (*b*) The transaction should be between Muslims and if either of the parties is a non-Muslim, he should at least enjoy rights equal to that of Muslims, that is, he should be a *dhimmi.*

The above-mentioned definition makes lawful all instances of *'riba'* in which a rich man takes loans to satisfy his luxurious urges or a trader takes loans to further his business or where a person places his savings in a bank or official saving organisation or a company or government department, and receives interest on that saving. The *Mawlana* considers all such dealings as *mudarabah,* commercial investment, or *ikra'* that is renting, which are all lawful.

Since this book refers to various kinds of *bay$^c$* and *riba* time and again, a chart is reproduced on the following page for the benefit of the readers.

(1 March 1936).

# VARIOUS
# COMMERCIAL DEALINGS
## and their rules

....................................................................................

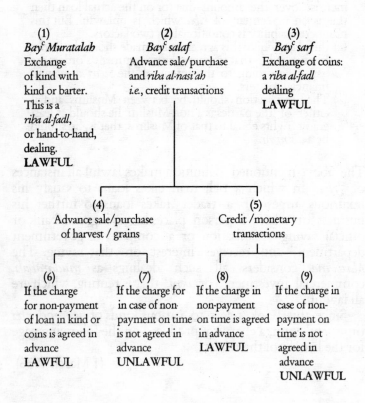

**(1)**
*Bay^c Muratalah*
Exchange
of kind with
kind or barter.
This is a
*riba al-fadl*,
or hand-to-hand,
dealing.
**LAWFUL**

**(2)**
*Bay^c salaf*
Advance sale/purchase
and *riba al-nasi'ah*
*i.e.*, credit transactions

**(3)**
*Bay^c sarf*
Exchange of coins:
a *riba al-fadl*
dealing
**LAWFUL**

**(4)**
Advance sale/purchase
of harvest / grains

**(5)**
Credit /monetary
transactions

**(6)**
If the charge
for non-payment
of loan in kind or
coins is agreed in
advance
**LAWFUL**

**(7)**
If the charge for
in case of non-
payment on time
is not agreed in
advance
**UNLAWFUL**

**(8)**
If the charge in
non-payment
on time is agreed
in advance
**LAWFUL**

**(9)**
If the charge in
case of non-
payment on
time is not
agreed in
advance
**UNLAWFUL**

*NB. Transactions 6th and 8th become unlawful
if the debtor is so poor that he is eligible for* sadaqah *and* Zakat.

# WHAT

# IS

# *RIBA*

# ?

## 1.

## Dichotomy of belief and practice
## regarding 'interest'[2]

In the Islamic community of India *sood*, or 'interest,' is generally regarded as synonymous with *riba*; that is the reason why Muslims in general consider all interest-based

---

2  A simplified transliteration scheme for Arabic, Persian and Urdu words and terms has been followed in this translation and a more exact transliteration has been avoided in order to ensure easy readability. However, <sup>c</sup> has been used for the Arabic <sup>c</sup>*ayn* (ع), *th* for *tha'* (ث), *i* for *ya'* (ی), *u* for the Arabic *waw* (و) and *oo* for the Urdu *waw* (ed.).

business, whatever be its nature, as proscribed ones. No doubt, if *sood*/'interest' and *riba* are synonymous, no Muslim can question the proscription of *riba* because the Holy Qur'an has clearly prohibited it.

Had practice been in accordance with the belief, there would have been no need for much probing and neither would there have been the need for the big debate on the issue raging these days on account of *Mawlana* Tufail Ahmad. But the fact remains that even religion did not remain unaffected by the general decadence that Muslims are going through since the downfall of their sovereignty in this country. As far as practices and morality are concerned, every aspect of our community life is deprived of the blessings of true religiosity. Take this very issue of *sood*/interest, for example. You will find that eighty per cent of those who believe in total proscription of *riba* or at least exhibit this faith are burdened with usuric debts, they have destroyed their properties or are losing them due to usury-based loans, whereas according to their own belief the one who pays *riba* is as much a sinner as the one who takes *riba* .[3]

The *Sahih Muslim, Abu Dawud* and *Sunan al-Tirmidhi* have all recorded the following *hadith*[4]:

لعن النبي صلى الله عليه وسلم آكلَ الربا وموكِله وشاهِدَه وكاتبه

---

[3]  *Mawlana* Shah ʿAbdul ʿAziz, *may his secret be sanctified*, has argued that the one who offers *riba* is a sinner for he offers the impure to others. But with due respect I would differ from this argument for 'eating *riba*' is forbidden for Muslims *only*, and therefore, offering it to those non-Muslims who believe in the propriety of *riba* will be lawful. But it is not so. Therefore, there must be some other reason. Let me mention that the taking of the *riba* forbidden in the *Shariʿah* is oppression and tyranny, and the offering of it is abetment of injustice, is because it has been forbidden in the Qur'an (5:2). Thus a Muslims' offering interest to a non-Muslim is a greater sin, for in that case a Muslim provides the opportunity to a non-Muslims to oppress Muslims.

Full reference citations of the Arabic works have been added at the end of each Arabic text. A list of the sources and editions used is appended to the book (ed.).

(صحيح الترمذي بشرح ابن العربي، ط. دار إحياء التراث العربي، بيروت ، ج
٥، ص ٢١٧ ؛ وبكلمات متقاربة في صحيح مسلم ، باب المساقاة، رقم
الحديث ١٠٦ ، ج ٥ ، ص ١٢١٩ ، ط. ٢ : اسطنبول ، ١٩٩٢ ؛ وسنن أبي
داؤد ، كتاب البيوع ، باب في أكل الربا ومؤكله ، ج ٣، ص ٢٤٤).

The Prophet (*pbuh*) cursed those who consume [take] *riba*,
and those who offer *riba* and its witness and its writer.

Another *hadith* says:

الآخذ والمعطي فيه سواء (صحيح النسائي، ج ٧، ص ٢٧٧)

In this [*riba*] both the giver and the taker are equal.

Pleaders file claims for *sood*/interest. Authorities issue
decrees for *sood*/interest. As long as the present British law
continues there seems no way to curb these evils. There is
no scope for escape from interest dealings in most trades. So
Muslims are compelled to indulge in interest dealings or
they have to surrender to competing rivals. Some people
think that the present economic backwardness of Muslims
is, to a large extent, due to this belief in the proscription of
interest, and it is due to this economic backwardness that
Muslims have fallen behind so much compared to their
fellow countrymen.

## 2.
## Disadvantages of the wrong definition of *sood*/interest

In these circumstances the following *hadith* of the Prophet
(*pbuh*) applies to us:

اليد العليا خير من اليد السفلى

21

(صحيح البخاري، كتاب الوصايا، باب تأويل قوله تعالى "من بعد وصية أو دين"، ج ٢، ص ٢٩٠، ط : ١، المطبعة السلفية ومكتبتها ، القاهرة، ١٤٠٣هـ).

The upper hand (the hand that gives) is better than the lower hand (the receiving hand).

It is extremely imperative to remove this economic deprivation of Muslims, and to look into the causes and reasons that have pushed us, as a community, to this state. As I have already mentioned, there are some people who mention the proscription of 'interest' as one of the big causes of Muslims' economic backwardness. They give the following reasons:

*a.* After believing in the unlawfulness of interest, there remains no incentive for savings and investment, for if there is no hope of an increase in the saved capital why should someone suppress desires in order to save money?

*b.* When the urge to save money recedes, the principles of frugality do not survive in life and extravagance becomes a habit. This is the real cause of the evil of senseless spending so rampant among Muslims.

*c.* First of all one needs a capital for starting a business. Later on, after having established a goodwill, big business transactions continue on credit, with even a small capital. As one has to deal with other communities in business one has to pay interest on his credit purchases. And when he sells on credit he must add at least that amount of interest which he himself has to pay, otherwise he will incur a loss instead of making a profit.

Avoidance of such dealings means losing a big source of livelihood. This is the reason why a very small numbers of Muslims are in the trading profession and this is the greatest cause of their poverty.

*d.* The interest-based business, that is banking, is itself a big commercial sector and as a result there are thousands of millionaires in other communities. But Muslims believe it to be forbidden and avoid it. The only few in interest-based business also believe in its unlawfulness, thus they intentionally and openly commit a sin and indulge in an impious act. Thus the reverence for religious commandments gradually diminishes.

e. The greatest drawback is that Muslims do not get loans when they need it from their Muslim brethren, for the Muslim capitalist does not believe in lending money on interest, then why should someone risk his money without expecting a profit. As a consequence, Muslims are compelled to borrow from others. Thus the fruits of our hard labour contribute to the economic progress of others and our wealth and properties are gradually shifting to others. Thriftiness and curbing the wants are prescribed for escaping such misfortunes.

Who says that thriftiness is not a commendable virtue? But the question is how to inspire thriftiness. While the rich in our community continue to be ridiculed as *Qaruns*.[5] As a result of paying two and a half percent *zakat* annually, capital continues to decline substantially, then who will forgo present pleasures for the sake of probable future wants. Thus ninety percent Muslims follow *Khawaja Shirazi*'s exhortation:

هنگام تنگدستي در عيش كوش ومستي
كاين كيميائے هستي قارون كند گدا را

Make merry and enjoy in adversity!
For this alchemy of life makes *Qarun* of the poor.

You may ask: is there no other use of money except the interest-based business? Why not invest the savings in a profitable business? But can everyone be a businessman? What should lawyers, physicians, employees and artisans do

---

5  *Qarun* (pronounced: *Qaaroon*) was an aide of the Pharoah of Egypt, contemporary to Moses. Identified as the Israelite 'Korah' of the *Bible* (Num. xvi:1-35; *cf.* the *Qur'an*, 28:76), he was supposed to have been the richest man of his time (ed.).

with their savings? If they invest it in a partnership business they will have to risk a loss as well. So who will invest to buy headache? However, all these cases relate to thrifty and rich people. There are no people in the world where all individuals are sagacious, thrifty, prudent and rich. In every class and every age human nature has varied and every society and people have the generous and the parsimonious; the frugal and the extravagant; the pauper and the rich: all sorts of people are found in every community. Sometimes quite a cautious and sagacious person is all of a sudden compelled to borrow in order to meet an inevitable need. So it is practically impossible that all individuals of the community remain safe from the misery of indebtedness.

Now the question arises: how can a Muslim get loans when he needs it. Rich Muslims, who have the capacity (to lend) are, after all, human; why should they give away their money to others in return for nothing. If they purchase land by the same money they can obtain land rent; if they build a house they can rent it; if they invest it in a business they can make a profit. But if they risk their capital and persuade themselves to lend it, they cannot get any return for the use of their money! Then why should they lend their money to anyone?

Lending money without *riba*, or *qard hasan* قرض حسن, may be a virtue, but even ʿ*ulama* do not believe it to be a virtue of a kind which is obligatory or one whose neglect is a sin. Moreover, there may be many other useful ways of promoting public good, more durable and noteworthy, than interest-free lending. In most cases of lending there are complaints instead of gratitude. There is a famous [Arabic] saying: القرض مقراض المحبة (debt is the scissors for love).

Thus rationally, or according to the *Shariʿah*, no Muslim capitalist can be compelled to lend money. There is no Islamic State where the *Baytul-mal,* state treasury, may meet the requirements of needy Muslims. In these circumstances Muslims are compelled to borrow from capitalists of other communities on interest. Thus, from the religious point of view, on the one hand, the Muslim borrower is compelled to get involved in this same 'sin' (*riba*) and, on the other

24

hand, there is an inevitable loss to the community, for in the repayment of the debt more than the original money will have to be paid and in case it remains unpaid, which happens in ninety-five percent cases, a Muslim family is destroyed only to become a source of increasing the wealth of another community. Had the same loan been given by a Muslim there would not have been any shortage in the overall wealth of the community despite the possible destruction of an individual Muslim. The process of progress and regress of individuals continues in every community and will continue. There is nothing special about it among Muslims. There is no dearth of short-sighted spendthrift people in other communities. Day in and day out thousands of families become destitute. Money itself is a shifting shadow — it is here today and there tomorrow:

وَتِلْكَ الأَيَّامُ نُدَاوِلُهَا بَيْنَ النَّاسِ (آل عمران : ١٤٠) .

And these are the days we revolve among people (3:140).

If we have gained something today, someone else has lost something. Naziri has penned this truth in his versified magical symphony:

زمانه گلشن عیش کرا به یغما داد
که گل به دامن ما دسته دسته می آید

Whose garden of pleasure has Time robbed?
For its flowers are coming to us bunch by bunch.

However, if the flowers of our garden are plucked so as to be used as bouquets to decorate our own rooms, we do not lose. The more a garden is plundered the more it adds to the splendour of the room. While a brother's pocket is emptied, another brother's is filled, and the community, as a whole, continues to own the same amount of wealth. For instance, if we decorate our room with flowers brought from someone else's garden, that is, if individuals of our community obtained capital, business, or interest or any other form of wealth, from another community, the capital of our community as a whole would continue to increase,

25

and in this way we would have economic superiority over the rival community. This is the criterion to adjudge a community rich or poor; otherwise, there is no dearth of hungry and homeless workers in a rich country like the United States and there are a few billionaires even among our poor Muslim community. But the question is not that of individuals but that of the community as a whole. And those who criticize the prohibition of interest do so from this very point of view: whatever be the condition of individuals, the community as a whole should be superior to others in every respect:

تن پہ تھا فاروق أعـظم کے پھٹا کرتا مگر
قوم کی خاطر بھري نیّت نہ لیکر ملك جم

Faruq the Great (ʿUmar) wore a torn shirt, but for the sake of his people he was not satisfied even after having conquered the Kingdom of *Jam* [Persia].

# 3.
# Studying the issue of *riba*

These are facts that cannot be overlooked and for this very reason the well-wishers of the community want to deeply probe the issue of *riba*. There are people who are bent upon justifying *sood*/interest with whatever excuse. But I want to assure you that whatever is stated in the forthcoming pages would be unaffected by such influences and would be a student-like study of the real issue. And with my limited knowledge and humble capacity, I will attempt to explain what could be a rational definition of *riba* according to the pronouncements of the *Shariʿah* and to what issues of the present age the term *riba* could be applied. A mention will be made of the terms the prohibition of *riba* has been conditioned with and whether these conditions obtain in India or not.

But before beginning the actual argument, it may be mentioned that Islam is an eternal law and its commandments are not bound by our changing opinions and limited wisdom, neither is it permissible to stretch the pronouncements of the *Shariah* unnecessarily so as to make it serve our own immature wisdom and our transient benefits. It is our prime duty to unquestionably submit to the mandates of the *Shariah* even if we have to surrender our dearest assets of life. Sacrifice is the first step towards martyrdom for the sake of the oneness of God, and every Muslim should always be prepared for it:

إِنَّ اللهَ اشْتَرَى مِنَ الْمُؤْمِنِينَ أَنْفُسَهُمْ وَأَمْوَالَهُمْ بِأَنَّ لَهُمُ الْجَنَّةَ (التوبة : ١١١).

Allah has purchased of the believers their persons and their wealth for theirs [in return] is Paradise (9:111).

متـــاع جان ودل دےکر رضائے حق خریدی ہے
یہ جھگڑا کب کا فیصل ہو چکا بیع وشراء ہو کر

We have bought God's pleasure
at the cost of life's treasures.
The issue has long been settled after that deal.

However, it is not proper to desist from rationality and wisdom while trying to understand the dictates of the *Shariah*, since it has been declared (in the Holy Qur'an itself):

أَفَلاَ يَتَدَبَّرُونَ الْقُرْآنَ (النساء : ٨٢ / محمد : ٢٤) .

Do they not ponder over the Qur'an (4:82/47:24).

It is our very belief that the brilliant Islamic *Shariah* takes care of all the religious and worldly interests and needs of its believers. The Holy Qur'an declares:

وَأَنْتُمُ الأَعْلَوْنَ إِنْ كُنْتُمْ مُؤْمِنِينَ (آل عمران : ١٣٩) .

You alone are the supreme [masters] if you are true in faith (3:139).

27

Then how could it be possible for the eternal and final law and the most complete of all faiths that any of its dictates go manifestly against rationality? Or why should the obedience to any of its dictates be a cause for the backwardness of Muslims in any walk of life? Or why its eternal laws would not contain special provisions for special circumstances? These are some premises that will be kept in mind while trying to understand the meaning of the injunctions of the *Shari'ah*.

# 4.
## Rational definitions of 'interest' and *riba*

If someone lends his capital temporarily to someone else in order to be used and to benefit from it, and while getting it back the creditor charges a fixed amount over and above the principal as a profit for the temporary possession of the money, this additional amount will be called 'interest' and its increase and decrease generally depends upon the duration of the temporary possession of the loan in the hands of the debtor.

In short, the fixed charge for the financial benefit is 'interest.' The purpose of borrowing is not debatable here, neither is the financial status of the borrower, his religious faith, or whether the place of the deal is an Islamic State or a non-Muslim State.

# 5.
## 'Interest' and *riba* are not synonymous

Now, let us see what *riba* means in the terminology of the Islamic *Shariʿah*. This much is certain that *'the riba'* الربا, according to the *Shariʿah*, and the commonly understood term of 'interest'/*sood* are not synonymous, for *ʿulama* have held certain definite forms of *riba* permissible. *Mawlana* ʿAbdul Hayy Lakhnawi and *Mawlana* Irshad Husayn Rampuri are among the undisputed pillars of the late period of the Hanafi *fiqh*. *Fatwas* of these esteemed scholars are found in the *Majmuʿa-i fatawa* by *Mawlana* ʿAbdul Hayy (vol. I, pp. 375, 394). A *fatwa* in this collection says that if someone buys goods for *rupees* one hundred in cash, in case of buying them on credit it is permissible for him to pay *rupees* one hundred and three after a month, *rupees* one hundred and six after two months and *rupees* one hundred and nine after three months. It adds that there is no harm in increasing the price by three *rupees* every month. Similarly, if someone gives a roll of cloth and in return gets two rolls of cloth of the same quality it is permissible in both cases, whether in hand-to-hand dealing or on credit for, in spite of being a commodity, it is not sold or purchased by *kayl* (measurement) or *wazn* (weight) (see *Fatawa-i Mawlana ʿAbdul Hayy*, p. 107).

Literally, *riba* ربا means a raise or increase. But it is absolutely certain that any raise or increase, or *riba*, is not *'the riba'* prohibited by the *Shariʿah*. Thus all the verses of the Holy Qurʾan regarding the prohibition of *riba* mention it as *'al-riba'* [*the riba*], that is, with the definite article *'al-'*. Certainly the definite article, *'al-'*, here is not indefinite or general, otherwise every form of monetary increase, such as business profit, would have been prohibited. So the *'al-'* here is specific and some special kind of increase has been prohibited under the *Shariʿah*. Let us see what is that special kind of increase. In the Holy Qurʾan itself neither is there any explicit description of that special sort nor is there any explicit definition of the word *riba*. So we must refer to the

*Hadith* to see if the Holy Prophet (*pbuh*) has defined it in any way. But the Prophet also did not explicitly define *riba*.

Imam Ahmad ibn Hanbal mentions the following *hadith* in his *Musnad* with reference to Faruq the Great (ʿUmar ibn al-Khattab):

إن آخر ما نزل من القرآن آية الربا وإن رسول الله صلى الله عليه وسلم قبض و لم يفسرها فدعوا الربا والرية (مسند احمد، مسند عمر بن الخطاب ، الحديث ٢٤٨ ، ج ١،ص ٦٠) .

The Qur'anic *ayah* regarding *riba* is the last part of the Qur'an revealed, and the Holy Prophet (*pbuh*) died before interpreting this *ayah*. So give up *riba* and anything that you doubt.

The *hadith* of Faruq the Great clarifies two things: one, apart from the literal meaning of the word, *riba* was applicable to a certain kind of a transaction, called *al-riba*, in those days; secondly, the Holy Prophet (*pbuh*) did not define the word *riba* in any way other than the then prevalent meaning of the term. It is the intention to show here that there is no saying of the Holy Prophet (*pbuh*) defining the word *riba*.

Among the four guiding sources of Islam, consensus إجماع stands third. Let us see if there is any consensus about the definition of *riba*. Here also the answer is in the negative. Strong differences are to be found among early authorities, from the *Sahaba* to the *Imams* of the *fiqhi* schools.

# 6.
## No consensus about the definition of *riba*

ʿAbdallah ibn ʿAbbas and ʿAbdallah ibn ʿUmar maintain that *riba* occurs only in credit dealings. Abu Saʿid al-

Khudari and ʿUbadah ibn al-Samit consider *riba* in hand-to-hand dealings also. ʿUbadah ibn al-Samit, during the course of a sermon, gave his verdict about *riba* in a certain case. When *Amirul Muʾminin* Muʿawiyah heard about it he wondered:

ألا ما بال رجال يتحدثون عن رسول الله صلى الله عليه وسلم أحـاديث؛ قد كنا نشهده ونصحبه فلـم نسمعها منه (صحيح مسلم ، كتاب المساقاة ، رقم الحديث ٨٠ ، ج ٢ ، ص ١٢١٠ ؛ وبكلمات متقاربة في صحيح النسائي ، كتاب البيوع ، ج ٧ ، ص ٢٧٦).

What is the problem with some people who speak of such narrations from the Prophet of Allah (*pbuh*). We used to witness him and keep his company but we never heard it from him.

*Imam* Dawud al-Zahiri considers *riba* in dealings of dates, barley, wheat, salt, silver and gold *only* and not in any other thing. *Imam* Malik applies *riba* only on storable edibles (مأكولات مدخرة), *i.e.*, those edible commodities that may be *stored*. Hanafis consider *riba* only in the exchange of commodities which are *weighable* (مكيل) and *measurable* (موزون) and that too only in *Dar al-Islam*. With Shafiʿis *edibility* طعمية and *value* ثمنية are the conditions.

The fact of the matter is that the narrations in this respect are themselves contradictory to each other. They will be discussed in detail at the appropriate occasion. We intended here to show through some examples that there is no consensus on the definition of '*riba*.'

Now, to define '*riba*' it is necessary to delve deeply into the Qurʾanic verses about *riba*. The circumstances of their revelation, their context, expediencies and the wisdom therein should be sincerely and faithfully investigated. As far as possible Qurʾanic interpretation should be done according to the hints found in the Holy Qurʾan itself. Whatever details could be found in the authentic *ahadith* of the Holy Prophet (*pbuh*), their reasons, rationale and circumstances should be traced. Thus whatever we can infer, according to our capacity, from Allah's and the Holy Prophet's (*pbuh*) commandments, shall be the basis to

31

formulate opinion about the contemporary issues. This is called inference قياس in the terminology of the *Shariʿah*.

Now, let us see what the considered opinion (*ijtihad*) of the early *Imams* about the definition of the *riba* is. Obviously, every *ijtihad* may not be necessarily correct and binding. The *Ummah* is unanimous that the *mujtahid imams* (may Allah's mercy be upon them) were not *maʿsum* (infallible). It is an accepted dictum that a *mujtahid* may commit a mistake and may be correct in the opinions he formulates (المجتهد يخطئ ويصيب). It is also obvious that the complications of monetary matters and varied situations recently created by contemporary civilization were not known during the auspicious period of the *mujtahid Imams*. Thus it will be a vain effort to look for the details of the contemporary issues in the books of *fiqh* (Islamic jurisprudence). But it is still quite necessary to go through the definition of *riba* by *fuqaha* (interpreters of Islamic law) and to examine it according to the criteria of the Holy Qur'an and the *Hadith*, rationality and tradition. If the definition of *riba*, given by the *fuqaha*, is true to that criterion and is applicable to the definition of *riba* then there is nothing like it. But if it is not applicable to the current meaning of 'interest' or if it is fundamentally against rationality or if it is contrary to the correct meaning and intent of the Holy Qur'an and *Hadith* and is based on incorrect inference, we must refer to the original source, that is, the Holy Qur'an and *Hadith*:

فَإِنْ تَنَازَعْتُمْ فِي شَيْءٍ فَرُدُّوهُ إِلَى اللهِ وَالرَّسُوْلِ (النساء: ٥٩).

If there is any dispute amongst you on any issue, refer it back to Allah and the Prophet (4:59).

# 7

# Definition of *riba* by Hanafi *Fuqaha*

The following is a summary of the definition of *riba* by the Hanafite *fuqaha*:

الربا محرم في كل مكيل أو موزون إذا بيع بجنسه متفاضلا، فالعلة عندنا الكيل مع الجنس أو الـوزن مع الجنس ... وعنـد الشـافعي الطعم في المطعومـات والثمنيـة في الأثمـان ... وإذا عـدم الوصفـان الجنـس والمعنـى المضموم إليه حل التفاضل والنساء... ويجوز بيع البيضة بالبيضتين، والتمرة بالتمرتين والجوزة بالجوزتين لانعدام المعيار ... والشافعي يخالفنا فيه لوجود الطعم ... ويجوز بيع الفلس بالفلسين بأعيانهمـا ... ولا يجـوز بيـع الحنطة بالدقيق ولا بالسويق، لأن المجانسة باقية من وجه لأنهما من أجزاء الحنطة، والمعيار فيهما الكيل، لكن الكيل غير مسو بينهما وبين الحنطة لاكتنازهما فيه وتخلخل حبات الحنطة ... ويجوز بيع الدقيق بالدقيق متساويا ... ويجوز بيع اللحم بالحيوان ... ويجـوز بيـع الخبـز بالحنطة والدقيق متفاضلا، لأن الخبز صار عدديا أو موزونا فخرج من أن يكـون مكيـلا ... ولا ربا بيـن المسلم والحربي (المرغيناني، الهداية، ط. كتب خانه رشيديه ، دهلي ، ب.ت. ، ج ٣، ص ٦١ - ٧٠) .

The *riba,* or increase, is prohibited in every measurable and weighable commodity if it is sold with an increase in a kind-for-kind transaction. The reason in our [Hanafis'] view is the transaction of kind-with-kind if it is measurable or weighable... According to *Imam* Shafi'i, the reason in edibles is their edibility and in valuables their value...

And if the two characteristics, kind and the attendant condition [weighability or measurability] are not found [in a transaction], it is lawful to deal with an increase or on credit... It is permissible to sell one *fils* [penny] for two *filses* in kind... It is not permissible to sell wheat for flour or mush because they belong to the same commodity, *i.e.,* they belong to wheat, which is measurable, yet they cannot be measured properly against each other because the flour and mush are in a condensed form while there is space between the grains of wheat... It is permissible to sell flour for flour in equal quantities... It is [also] permissible to sell meat against animal... And it is permissible to sell bread against wheat or flour with an increase, because the bread is sold in numbers or by weight and therefore it is no longer measurable... There is no *riba* between a Muslim and a *harbi*.[6]

---

[6] *'Harbi'* حربي is a resident of *dar al-harb, i.e.,* non-Muslim country. This point will be explained later in this book (ed.).

# 8.
## Kayl and bayᶜ explained

In the foregoing quotation 'kayl' كيـل is translated as 'measure' and 'bayᶜ' بيـع as 'sale' or transaction. Thus some people may have difficulty in understanding the true connotations of these words. Therefore, it is necessary to explain them here.

'Kayl' does not mean all sorts of measurements such as yard, feet etc. In fact, 'kayl' was a kind of basket which was used as a measure in the sale and purchase of commodities. Similarly the word 'bayᶜ' may mean only "sale" to some people. But in Arabic language this word has a wide connotation and it is applicable to all types of trading. Sometimes it is applicable to all kinds of financial matters. For example, barter is bayᶜ muratalah بيع مراطلة, advance buying is bayᶜ salaf بيع سلف, exchange of coins is bayᶜ sarf صرف بيع, that is, sarrafah صرافة (exchange of currencies). The Holy Qur'an says:

إِذَا نُودِيَ لِلصَّلوةِ مِنْ يَّوْمِ الْجُمُعَةِ فَاسْعَوْا إِلَى ذِكْرِ اللهِ وَذَرُوا الْبَيْـع

(الجمعة: ٩).

And when the adhan is proclaimed on Fridays, [calling] for prayers, run towards the remembrance of Allah and stop every "bayᶜ" (trading) (62:9).

You have seen the definition of riba as given by the Hanafi fuqaha, in the words of the author of the Hidayah. We will see later whether this definition itself is right or wrong. At present we have to see how far it is applicable to the present-day interest-based business. Let me say that this definition applies to the transactions in [Indian] villages where cereals are lent on the condition that the loan-in-kind will be repaid with an increase of a quarter or a half, provided that the repayment is, for instance, barley-for-barley. But if barley is exchanged with wheat or rice, or if the deal is made with any other commodity or a cash amount is fixed, it will not be riba according to the Hanafis, be it a direct transaction or on credit.

34

As for cash [against cash] transactions, they will be permissible even if the commodity is exchanged for commodity, for, there is no *kayl* [measure] nor weight involved in such transactions, instead they are counted and their amount is fixed by counting [not by *kayl* or weight].

As the author of the *Hidayah* has said, one *fils* [coin] may be exchanged for two *filses* in kind, and the exchange of bread and flour in excess or in a lesser quantity is permissible. It is not so because some labour is included in the case of bread. Had it been so, trading in wheat and flour would have been similarly permissible. But according to the author of the *Hidayah*, the reason for permissibility is that the flour is sold by basket-measure and the bread is sold by counting or by weight. Thus a Hanafi can be at ease with all sorts of interest-based trades. Only in some instances will he have to juggle a little with words, such as, taking *rupees* in exchange for guineas [gold coins] or currency notes, or taking a smaller silver coin and some smaller coins in exchange for a silver *rupee*, and so on.

Now it is clear that the present-day interest-based business, and *the riba* are completely different from each other. The Hanafis, at least, have no right to have any objection to the contemporary interest-based business.

## 9.
## Increment of commodity is not *riba*

It may be said here that the foregoing definition of *riba* in the *Hidayah* is applicable only to *riba al-fadl*, that is, increase by one party in hand-to-hand dealings, and that *riba al-nasi'ah*, that is credit with interest, is different from it. In that case [*riba-al-nasi'ah*], any increment is *riba* irrespective of the sameness of the commodity and without the condition of *kayl* and weight. But this is not correct.

The author of the *Hidayah* has not given separate definitions of the *riba-al-fadl* and *riba al-nas'iah* and this is rational. If *riba* occurs in both cases of cash and credit, then whatever the definition of *riba*, it will be common in both cases. This is the reason why the author of the *Hidayah* has, without any specification, given a single definition of *riba* for both cases, that is regarding 'commodity' as the logical reason [for *riba*] in commodity transactions, and "*fadl*" [increment] in the transactions of commodities by *kayl* and weight. It is mentioned in the *Majmuʿa-i fatawa-i Mawlana ʿAbdul Hayy* مجموعه فتاوى مولانا عبد الحي (vol. 3, p. 107):

علّت تحريم ربا چيست ؟

والجواب : كيل يا وزن يا اتحاد جنس اگر هر دو معلوم اند همچون بيع يك تهان با دو تهان پارچه هم تفاضل حلال است وهم نساء ...

What is the reason for the prohibition of *riba*?

The reply is: "*kayl*", or weight, or the sameness of the commodity. And if both of these are non-existent in the two commodities, it is permissible to exchange two rolls of cloth [which is not sold by measure as explained above or weight] with one roll, with an increase or on credit.

But the question is: whether the *riba* so assiduously forbidden in the Holy Qur'an and the perpetrator of which has been described as one at war with God and His Prophet (*pbuh*), is the same thing as defined by Hanafi *fuqaha* in the foregoing lines? I would say "no, certainly not". My arguments are as follows:

*a.* First of all, this definition covers hand-to-hand deals also and there can be no *riba* in hand-to-hand deals for, the parties freely make the deal and exchange their commodities by mutual understanding. Each party is equally needy and equally free; none of them has any superiority over the other. Here the situation is not that of lending where one party is needy and the other is carefree and contented. In hand-to-hand dealings the two parties enjoy equal status and there is no question of favour or obligation; thus there is no scope for compulsion or cheating or undue influence. If there is an increase or decrease in the quantity of the exchanged commodities, then the quality of the two commodities also varies. In such deals every party, in its view, will receive equivalent-in-price commodities. Thus both parties will be at par in profit and loss. Here there is no apprehension as well that the moral responsibility of helping the needy, obviously falling upon the rich, has been neglected.

However, if both parties have the same commodity of the same value then there should not be any reason for exchange, neither has such an exchange ever taken place. There must be some kind of difference in the commodities in the case of hand-to-hand exchange. An equal exchange of unequal commodities is unnatural. So there is no need for such a rule in the first place, because such exchanges do not occur and even if they do, to act according to such rules will be against human nature:

لاَ يُكَلِّفُ اللهُ نَفْساً إِلاَّ وُسْعَهَا (البقرة : ٢٨٦) .

On no soul doth Allah place a burden greater than it can bear (2:286).

The application of *riba* on hand-to-hand dealings will be a slander against the *Shariʿah* of Allah. Moreover, the application of *riba* on hand-to-hand dealings will be clearly against the authentic *ahadith* that clearly state:

لا ربا إلا في النسيئة (صحيح البخاري ، كتاب البيوع ، فتح الباري، ج ٤، ص ٣٠٣).

There is no *riba* except in *nasi'ah* [credit dealings].

التمر بالتمر ربا إلا هاء وهاء (صحيح البخاري، كتاب البيوع، باب بيع التمر بالتمر، فتح الباري، ج ٤، ص ٣٠٠).

[Exchange of] dates with dates is *riba* except in hand-to-hand dealings.

لا ربا إلا في الدَّين: There is no *riba* except in debt [credit].

b. What does the linking of *riba* with the kind-to-kind exchange of commodities mean? It is strange that taking five kilograms and a quarter of barley in exchange for five kilograms of barley is forbidden but taking ten kilograms of wheat in exchange for the same five

37

kilograms of barley is perfectly *halal* and pure! Is this game of words called the *Shariʿah*? Moreover, the definition of kind/commodity has been extended to such an extent that the commonality of *name* is sufficient to bring it into the gambit of *riba*. Rice selling at five kilograms for a *rupee* or the *basmati* variety selling at one kilogram for a *rupee* and tobacco selling at two kilograms for a *rupee* or its special variety selling at eighty *rupees* per kilogram are all equal. Not only this, manufactured goods and the raw materials used in their production are all treated on an equal footing. For example, a gold biscuit and a studded golden chain are one commodity, and wheat, flour and bread are regarded as belonging to the same commodity.

If this inference is correct, the religion that does not waste the reward of anyone, in this case holds the wasting of reward as obligatory. For example, if someone gives five kilograms of wheat and takes back four and a half kilograms of flour and gives wheat in a greater quantity in order to pay for the charges of grinding, both the poor labourer and the good-mannered customer have committed the sin of *riba* and both of them are enemies of Allah and the Holy Prophet (*pbuh*).

This was the inference of the early *fuqaha*. Some contemporary ʿ*ulama* have gone farther. In modern civic life gold and silver are mere commodities, they have nothing to do with cash or pricing, neither are they used as cash for price standardization; on the contrary guinea, *rupee*, *paisa*, *ikannis* [one sixteenths of a *rupee*], *chawannis* [one fourth of a *rupee*] and currency notes are mere cash, they are not used as commodities neither can they be used as such, otherwise a paper currency having face value ranging from five to one thousand *rupees*, may, as a *commodity* [paper] be costly even for a single *paisa*. Or for a *chawanni*, made of nickel, one can buy nickel many times in weight. However, one thing is clear that coins only represent a value standardized by a certain government, otherwise their face value and intrinsic value are not related to each other. Thus to consider a *rupee* and silver as one and same commodity would

38

amount to proclaiming one's own ignorance. The difference between the fixed cash price and the market value has been prevalent since ancient times. That is why in ancient Persia coins were called 'shahrawa' شَهْرَوَا (that is a coin introduced by the State). A famous verse of Sa‘di supports us:

بزرگ زاده نادان بشهروا ماند
که در دیار غریش بهیچ نستانند

A great man's silly son went unrecognized
in a foreign land;
He became like a coin
which has no takers outside its kingdom.

However, one of our contemporary *ulama* decrees that buying silver from market greater in weight than the weight of a *rupee* amounts to consuming *riba*. But does the *Mawlana* consider this deal as forbidden? No. While the definition of commodity has been expanded to the point where silver nugget and the [silver] *rupee* are one and same commodity, the trick to circumvent this holy *talisman* has also been spelt out. It is this: to avoid loss, buy one and a quarter *tola* of silver for a silver *rupee* in such a way that you pay various silver coins for fourteen *annas* [a *rupee* had sixteen *annas*] such as *athanni* (eight *annas*), *chawanni* (four *annas*), *duwanni* (two *annas*) and pay the balance in *paisas* and say that you bought one *tola* of silver for 14 *annas* and the rest for eight *paisas*. At the time of uttering this, will your heart too concur with your tongue? Can there be a worse example than this of trying to deceive one's own self as well as Allah? In other words, does this not mean that if the sin of *riba* is compounded by lying to Allah, then the two sins will together become a pious act? Is this playing with words and deception with faith called the *Shari‘ah*? God forbid!

A learned and enlightened friend has written a comprehensive article on the prohibition of interest. He has

---

[7] *Tola* is a an Indian weight equal to 180 grains (about 12 grams) (ed.)..

39

attempted to prove through rational arguments that the person who charges interest does not do any benevolence to the needy person but charges for helping him in his distress, and, instead of any financial exchange, takes a little more money than the original sum, that this is why *riba* in forbidden under the *Shari'ah*.

It will be seen later how far this argument is correct. Here the question arises that if the definition of *riba*, as given by *fuqaha*, is accepted as correct, then how the objective, which is the intent of the law-giver, as the *Mawlana* says, can be attained? I would rather submit that the conditioning of *riba* with the exchange of kind-for-kind will legalize all kinds of piracy simply through the change of commodity. Perhaps the *Mawlana* himself stumbled at this rationale, so elsewhere only to rationalize the condition of the exchange of a commodity with commodity he has attempted to present the rational argument that the exchange of commodities does not help promote civilization and therefore it is forbidden by the *Shari'ah*. First of all, he himself does not believe that the exchange of commodities is forbidden, he holds only the excess as improper. Moreover, this disparity in exchange of commodities will continue; for example, a farmer having no cash wants to sow small peas but he has no seeds. He has large, *kabuli*, peas in excess of his need and his neighbour has an excess of small peas and he is prepared exchange it with the *kabuli* peas. Now, both of them do exchange as per their need but this exchange was done weight for weight without any consideration for the *value* of the respective peas. Now tell me whether the owner of the *kabuli* peas was a loser or not? Had the poor man possessed money or had he lived near a market place, he would have purchased the small peas at the rate of eight *annas* (50 *paisas*) per kilogram and would have sold his *kabuli* peas at the rate of twelve *annas* (75 *paisas*) a kg.. The poor farmer was a looser because of your *fatwa*, but what has civilization gained through this deal? And had there been a deal with an increase according to the value (of the respective commodities), what loss would have civilisation suffered? And lastly, why should the view of the said *Mawlana*, that

40

the exchange of a commodity with commodity with an increase has no benefit for civilisation, be accepted as correct? I. would rather submit that the contrary is correct, for, if the increase is held as improper then there will be no incentive for producing goods of better quality. Moreover, from the prohibition of *muratalah*, that is, exchange of commodity with commodity, how can it be concluded that the increase in that case is *riba*. There could be other reasons for prohibition which will be stated later. However, our *Mawlana*, having himself realized the weakness of his argument, did not rest at that but offered another argument that if the increase in the exchange of commodity-with-commodity is permitted, all the quantity of a certain commodity would be accumulated with one single person. Can anyone understand the meaning of this statement? Had it been the objective of the *Shari'ah* that any commodity should not be allowed to be accumulated with a single person, then *muratalah* should have been made compulsory rather than being forbidden for, in case of *muratalah* the dealing parties will have the same commodity, and if *muratalah* is forbidden and sale against coins is permitted, as it is mentioned in the *hadith* itself, then a rich person could buy that commodity from everywhere and become the sole owner of that commodity.

The argument offered by the *Mawlana* goes against himself. Moreover, the term 'commodity' itself is quite ambiguous. For example, cereal is a commodity which includes barley, wheat, gram etc.; or food is a commodity which includes all animal and vegetable edibles. And if you say that cereal is not a commodity but wheat is a commodity then why don't you say, likewise, that *basmati* rice and an inferior quality rice are two different commodities. Mere commonality of the word "rice" simply does not make them the same commodity. Then how come [the *fiqhi* principle which says] إن جيدها ورديها سواء 'Its good and bad [varieties] are same'? We are supported by other authentic *ahadith* also. See, for instance, those that say that 'except those whose colours are different; except those whose varieties are different':

41

"إلا ما اختلفت ألوانها"، "وإلا ما اختلفت أصنافها" (صحيح مسلم ،
كتاب المساقاة ، باب الصرف وبيع الذهب بالورق نقدا، رقم الحديث ٨٣ /
١٥٨٨ ، ج ٢، ص ١٢١١ ؛ و النسائي ، كتاب البيوع ، باب بيع التمر
بالتمر، ج ٧ ، ص ٢٧٣ – ٢٧٤).

This obviously means that if goods of similar commodity differ in quality then the exchange of commodities with an increase will be permissible.

Surprisingly, on the one hand, the definition of 'commodity' is so expanded and generalised that, without any consideration for value or quality, mere *commonality* of name is considered sufficient for the attribution of a single commodity, and, on the other hand, equality has been interpreted as equality in quantity instead of equality of quality. Consequently the conclusions under *fiqh* drawn from the assemblage of these two mistakes are surprising. It is said that if you exchange one kilogram of sugar for two kilograms of jaggery, one kilogram of jaggery taken in excess of the quantity of sugar comes under *riba*, for both belong to the commodity of 'sugar' and any increase in the exchange of this commodity [being sold by weight] is *riba*. This is like saying: 'all big and small carry the same price tag.'

For God's sake, do consider if such tenets can be implemented in any age? Will someone like to give the best quality gold and in return accept an inferior quality gold of equal weight? Or will someone give an engraved silver scent-case and accept silver of equal weight in return? Then what is the need for such unpracticable tenets? Even if there is such a single silly person among millions of people, would not such a deal amount to suicide on the one side and cruelty and usurpation of rights on the other? Can a revealed *Shariʿah* order piracy in the name of faith? By God, may the excommunicators bite the dust, I am prepared to say that such unnatural and senseless tenets can never be the intent of the *Shariʿah*. The faith and high regard that every Muslim holds for the Holy Prophet, for whom I sacrifice my father and mother, can never stoop to attribute such irrational and cruel tenets to the Holy Prophet and thus make Islam a target of condemnation.

c. In the foregoing definition of *riba*, according to *fiqh*, most notable is the condition of *kayl* (measure) and weight. In fact, *kayl* and weight are two different methods of the same act. As mentioned earlier, *kayl* was a basket-like measure, used for the sake of convenience for weighing goods for the sale and purchase of commodities. Milkmen still sell milk in this way. First they weigh a specific quantity of milk in a pot and show that the pot holds a certain quantity of milk, then they continue to sell milk by measuring it in the same pot. Thus *kayl*, in fact, is also a weight.

Now, as for the question of weight, it means in the first place that the particular commodity should be weighable. The second meaning may be that that commodity is *generally* sold *by weight* in the market. Taking the meaning in the first sense, everything in the world is weighable due to gravity. So an increase in anything is *riba*! Now even air and light can be weighed. If the said principle is accepted, doing two acts of benevolence in return for one such act will also be improper, for benevolence is a human act and a human act is weighable! Denial of this principle will certainly amount to the denial of the Weighing Scale on the Day of Judgement, which is the creed of the Mu<sup>c</sup>tazilites. Thus in the case of the said two acts of benevolence in return for one act of benevolence, there are all the needed elements: commodity, *kayl* and increment! Now what is short of *riba* in it? Suppose this is not real *riba*, yet it does resemble *riba*, so avoidance is imperative in accordance with [<sup>c</sup>Umar's saying]: فدعوا الربا والريبة (give up *riba* and every doubtful act).

This was just an interesting hypothetical case. But it cannot be denied that weight does not mean weighability, for the author of the *Hidayah* has held the deal of flour for bread with an increase as proper while he accepts that flour and bread belong to the same commodity. His argument for the justification of this deal is the same, that is: despite its weighability, flour is sold by measuring it by basket and bread is sold by count or by weight. So it must be

43

recognized that *kayl* and weight do not mean measurability and weighability but the *tradition* of measure and weight in respect of a certain commodity. For example, in the days of the author of the *Hidayah* wheat or flour were sold by basket measures, so in his view that deal was improper because in that measure the quantity must be in excess or less. Wheat grains being separate leave a lot of empty space and they are less in quantity in the measuring basket, contrarily flour particles stick together so the same measure bears a greater quantity of the flour. But this deal with equal weight will be 'proper' today for the tradition of selling by basket is defunct, because flour is sold by weight not by measuring baskets. On the contrary, if bread begins to be sold by weight, then today the exchange of bread with flour with an increase will be unlawful although the author of the *Hidayah* held it proper because in his days flour was sold by measuring in baskets and bread by count.

Thus it seems that the precepts of the *Shari'ah* are subject to our temporary traditions and to the outward appearance of our transactions. Mangoes and guavas are sold by count in Benares [Varanasi], but smaller mangoes in Aligarh and guavas in Azamgarh are sold by weight. Thus in Benares barter deal of mango and guava with an increase is proper but the deals of smaller mangoes in Aligarh and of guava in Azamgarh with an increase will be *riba!* For God's sake, is this the religion that claims eternal guidance for the whole world?

Moreover, if *kayl* and weight are necessary conditions of *riba* and that is the reason for *riba*, as mentioned by the author of the *Hidayah* and *Mawlana* 'Abdul Hayy Lakhnawi (ra), the dealings of commodities that are not sold by *kayl* or weight will not be *riba* according to the Hanafi *fiqh*. For example, if a poor person buys a roll of cloth on credit for the coffin of his mother and the trader gives it to him on the condition that he will take two rolls of cloth in return, then it is a completely lawful and proper deal (see *Fatawa-i-Mawlana 'Abdul Hayy*). He says that taking two rolls of cloth in return for one roll in cash or on credit are both proper. Similarly the house-building timber, which is sold neither by basket nor by weight but according to cubic feet, and thousands of things of daily use that are sold by the dozen or by score, when given can be taken back in double or triple quantity and it will be proper. The most interesting thing is that cash, such as, *rupee, paisa, ikannis, chawannis,* currency notes, all of them are neither subject to *kayl* nor weight, then why getting back two *rupees* after having given one *rupee* is improper?

d. There is no ethical, social, cultural or economic justification for qualifying *riba* on *kayl* or weight or regarding these attributes as the *justification* for *riba,* although no precept of the excellent *Shari°ah* can be without expedience and wisdom. Moreover, there is no *shar°i* argument about *kayl* and weight and exchange of commodity with commodity. Rather, it is the result of wrong inference, as you will see in the discussion on the *Hadith.*

e. In the foregoing definition the position(s) of the parties involved and the purpose(s) and nature of their dealings have not been taken into consideration; all have been treated equally although position(s) of contracting parties vary in the matter of credits and trade and there should be different rules for both of them. Similarly, the positions of the individuals in the case, and the purpose of the deal itself, should have affected the rules. For instance, a poor man buys cereals on credit to feed his family during famine; another person borrows money in order to deposit it for a demand in a court decree in exercise of his right of pre-emption *(shuf°ah)*; a third person needs money to buy a huge lot of commercial commodities at a cheap rate in an auction and hopes to earn twice or four times higher profit. In the afore-mentioned definition (of *riba*) the personal status of the three individuals has not been taken into consideration. But our faith is never prepared to accept that the Holy Qur'an and the Holy Prophet *(pbuh)* would not have taken these conditions into consideration.

*f.* The above discussion must have enlightened every just and right-thinking person to realise that the definition of *riba* given by the author of the *Hidayah* does not seem to be proper. Even then, by putting at the end the condition that لا ربا بين المسلم والحربي (there is no *riba* between the resident of *Dar al-harb* (non-Muslim country) and a Muslim resident of *Dar al-Islam* (Muslim State)), he has compensated to some extent. Rationality too demands it, for whatever be the logical definition of *riba*, its prohibition is a cultural and social injunction which can be imposed on the followers of Islam only in their dealings in an Islamic State. Wherever Islamic tenets are not in force in social matters, *riba* should be permissible in the dealings with non-Muslims. A detailed discussion about this will be attempted at the appropriate place. However, except the condition mentioned above, and irrespective of whatever some <sup>c</sup>*ulama* may have said, the above definition of *riba* is not rationally correct.

Now, let us see to what extent the *Shari<sup>c</sup>ah* support this *fiqhi* inference.

# 10.
## Some principles about the reliability of *hadiths*

*Fuqaha*'s inference of the definition of *'riba'* is not based on the Holy Qur'an for therein there is not the slightest description not even a hint of the 'principles' laid down by *fuqaha'* like commodity-for-commodity or weight or *kayl* or edibility or price value. The whole structure of this *fiqhi* argument is based on the narrations of *Hadith*. Moreover, most people, in spite of claiming to be Hanafites, argue for the prohibition of *riba* on the basis of these narrations. Therefore, we shall discuss them in some detail, and in this connection we shall take a critical look at the definition of *riba* offered by Shafiᶜis and Malikis.

But before referring to the actual narrations, it is imperative to mention some principles as a matter of foreword.

(a) *Muhaddithun*, may Allah bless them, have laboured extremely hard in the narration of *Hadith* and have established many principles and methods about the art of narration. They have mentioned about each and every narrator how far he is authentic, quality of his memory, from whom he has narrated, who were his contemporaries and where his narrations stand according to the rules of narration. They have accumulated an unlimited mass of material on the art of narration and the history of narrators. However, *muhaddithun* were human and fallible. It is quite likely that some authentic *ahadith* were not upto their criteria of critical scrutiny and judgement and thus they are not available today or they were considered weak or fabricated *ahadith*. Similarly, it is quite likely that a narrator considered by the *muhaddithun* as authentic and having a good memory, in fact might not be so. Or, in spite of having a good memory, he might have made an incorrect narration and thus a wrong narration could have been included among the authentic ones.

(b) Most of the narrations are derivations [*i.e.*, not quotes of actual words], that is, the actual words of the Holy Prophet (*pbuh*) have not been quoted in the narration and whatever the narrator understood to be the meaning of the Prophet's (*pbuh*) words, according to his capacity and capability, he narrated with the best of intention as the saying of the Holy Prophet (*pbuh*). Now, everyone knows that besides words even the slightest change in the style of delivery can induce a great difference in the meaning.

47

*(c)* At times the Holy Prophet (*pbuh*) gave two different instructions on two different occasions and the two had many words in common but they were of different nature, but the narrator mixed up the two by mistake, juxtaposing words of one instruction into the other instruction. And thus, due to a slight change in the actual narration, the meaning changed completely.

*(d)* Sometimes the Holy Prophet (*pbuh*) gave a brief instruction and did not mention any reason for it. Now the listener made up the 'reason' for this instruction according to his mental capacity. As the process of narration proceeded further the narrator's addition became part of the original *hadith*. Then on the basis of this expanded narration, some esteemed persons from amongst the *sahaba* or from the subsequent generation, *tabi'in*, issued a *fatwa* in a certain case according to his understanding, and after sometime this *fatwa* also becomes part of the *hadith*. See how far off the mark things go and how much the real meaning is distorted. When *fuqaha* got this narration after it had undergone so many changes they started logical hair-splitting but they did not make any attempt to enquire about the authenticity of a narration themselves in order to cleanse it of the superfluities.

*(e)* Sometimes we find a narration which is totally irrational or against the Qur'anic text or against the greatness of the Holy Prophet (*pbuh*). Such narrations can never be acceptable, however authentic their narrators may be. Instead of attributing such narrations to the Holy Prophet (*pbuh*), it would be more appropriate to consider them as the misunderstanding of the narrator, for the narrators were, after all human and, however high the status in holiness they might enjoy, there is the possibility of misunderstanding on their part, for all the followers of *Sunnah* agree that infallibility is an honour specific to the Holy Prophet (*pbuh*).

The belief in the infallibility of narrators is not an injunction of the *Shariʿah*. And according to our belief, it is impossible that any order of the Holy Prophet (*pbuh*) could be irrational or against the words and the spirit of the Holy Qur'an. Moreover, piety and holiness are different from the capacity to comprehend issues, and the ability to convey their correct meanings to others is yet another quality and their combination is not necessarily found in one person. But surprisingly enough, in spite of all this, a mistake in the research of *muhaddithun* or in the wordings of narrators is not considered tenable even if some narrations differ from other narrations or from the verse(s) of Holy Qur'an, and even if the acceptance of such narrations invites objections to the true faith of Islam itself and despite the behaviour of the blessed *sahaba*, may Allah be pleased with them, who did not hesitate to reject such *ahadith*. For example, we all know that when Abu Hurayrah, may Allah be pleased with him, narrated that the dead are punished when the bereaved cry, Mother of the Faithful (*Umm al-Mu'minin*) ʿAyisha *Siddiqah* [the Truthful], may Allah be pleased with her, admonished him and reminded him that Allah Himself has said (no وَلَا تَزِرُ وَازِرَةٌ وِزْرَ أُخْرَى (الأنعام : ١٦٤) one carries the burden of someone else — 6:164) then how could it be possible that the dead are punished when the bereaved cry, that is, another person is punished instead of the perpetrator of the sins? This can never be the saying of the Holy Prophet (*pbuh*). In fact what happens is that while relatives cry in bereavement, the dead person grapples with the consequences of his actions. This is the fact which the Holy Prophet (*pbuh*) had mentioned. Due to a misunderstanding, the narrator introduced a cause and effect relationship between the crying and the punishment.

Several other similar incidents have been described by ʿAyisha *Siddiqah* and other *sahaba*. Now, suppose that a lady like ʿAyisha *Siddiqah*, the most learned in *fiqh* among Muslim women, had not been present

49

there and the narration had been left unchallenged, what a blemish it would have been on the face of Islam!

By mentioning these incidents it is not intended to make *ahadith* doubtful and reject them as result, and be oblivious of the great treasure that we possess today due to the praiseworthy efforts of the *muhaddithun*, a great part of which is the most correct collection of the sayings and deeds of the Holy Prophet (*pbuh*) and his actions, and thus destroy a great pillar of our faith. The objective is to be careful before accepting a strange *hadith* as authentic. We should not be content with the principles of narration only, but, keeping in mind the above mentioned possibilities, it should be compared with other narratives on the subject with similar meaning or context, and should be considered in view of the Qura'nic verses and wisdom of faith. If a narration is correct according to all these criteria, then who can doubt that it is obligatory?

## 11.
## Kinds of narrations and their examples

In view of the foregoing discussion, the narrations which are used by *fuqaha* in their argument for *riba*, are of two categories[8]:

---

8   The blessed *muhaddithun* themselves differentiated between the narrative methods by ʿ*an* عن (from/on the authority of) and *haddathana* حدثنا (narrated to us). But this only means that on the basis of their findings, which could have been based, at the most, on narrators' reports; *muhaddithun* specifically used the word *haddathana* for the narrations which they did not find as literal quotations. But however venerable the research of the

(1) In the first category are those narratives which, while describing a certain event, quote the Holy Prophet's sayings in affirmative or negative terms. These are more likely to be correct and most probably they may contain some words actually spoken by the Holy Prophet (*pbuh*) himself.

(2) In the second category are those narratives that do not describe any incident or action — but the narrator, according to his own understanding, narrated the Holy Prophet's (*pbuh*) orders in plain and informative sentences. So in all probability, such narratives are derived and thus they are of a lesser degree of importance in comparison with those of the first category. And, as such, narrations are the results of the narrators' inference, so further inferences from them are more likely to have mistakes.

Those of the first category also have two definitions: one, those the time and the occasion of issuing of which are known and fixed, and, second, those the occasion of which is not known. Thus those narrations are most preferable in which the Holy Prophet's (*pbuh*) action or instruction about any occurrence is mentioned and the occasion and the time of issuing instructions are known. Even among these most reliable are those narrations which contain

---

*muhaddithun* may be, they are not revelations or divine inspirations compelling us to believe in them as a religious duty. So apart from the research about the method of narration, it is imperative to go into the wordings of the *hadith* itself in order to find out which instruction is literal and which one is indirect (interpreted). In our humble opinion, all narrations in simple statement-like sentences which state general principles, are mostly direct quotations. Only a few *ahadith* could be exempted from this rule like: إنما الأعمال بالنيات (Verily actions are according to intentions), or من سكت سلم ومن سلم نجا (whoever kept silent was spared and whoever was spared, saved). So taking this principle into consideration, I have classified the narratives of the *ahadith* and accordingly classified the narrations and did not confine myself to observing the rules laid down by the blessed *muhaddithun*.

maximum details, because narrations that do not contain details are subject to doubt that the details left out by the narrator by mistake or due to misunderstanding might have been the real cause of the Holy Prophet's (pbuh) order.

Now we are going to mention the narrations of the first and second categories, in that order, which have been used by *fuqaha* in their arguments about *riba*. First of all those will be mentioned which in our view are not related to *riba* and then those that are really related to *riba* or go towards clearly supporting our inference in defining the meaning of *riba*.

## (a) The first narration

Abu Saʿid al-Khudari and Abu Hurayrah narrate that:

إن رسول الله صلى الله عليه وسلم استعمل رجلا على خيبر فجاءهم بتمر جنيب، فقال : أكلّ تمر خيبر هكذا ؟ فقال : إنا لنأخذ الصاع من هذا بالصاعين والصاعين بالثلاثة . فقال : لا تفعل ! بِع الجمعَ بالدراهم ثم ابتع بالدراهم جنيبا (صحيح البخاري، كتاب الوكالة، باب الوكالة فى الصرف والميزان، فتح الباري ، ج ٤ ، ص ٣٧٩) ؛ وقد وردت روايات مماثلة فى البخاري، كتاب المغازي، باب استعمال النبي على أهل خيبر، فتح الباري، ج ٧ ، ص ٤٠٠، وكتاب الاعتصام ، باب إذا اجتهد العامل أو الحاكم فأخطأ خلاف الرسول من غير علم فحكمه مردود، فتح الباري، ج ١٣، ص ٢٧٠؛ وصحيح مسلم، كتاب المساقاة ، رقم الحديثين ٩٤ - ٩٥، ج ٢، ص ١٢١٥) .

The Holy Prophet (pbuh) appointed a person as governor of Khaybar. He came to the Holy Prophet (pbuh) and brought *Janib* dates with him. The Holy Prophet (pbuh) asked if all the dates of Khaybar are of the same kind. The official said: "no, we buy <u>one *saʿ*[9] of these dates for two *saʿs*</u> of ordinary dates and two *saʿs* of these dates with three *saʿs* of ordinary dates." The Holy Prophet (pbuh) said "do not

---

[9] *Saʿ* صاع , an Arab cubic measure, is equal to 5.33 pints in the Hijaz and 8 pints in Iraq (Lane, *Arabic-English Lexicon*) (ed.).

do so, but sell ordinary dates for coins and then buy these dates with coins."

Now see for yourselves what has this narration to do with *riba*? Nowhere is *riba* mentioned in the whole *hadith*, neither this order can be considered as a law-making rule. When he heard about a matter, the Prophet spoke about a better method to deal with it and warned about a mistake in calculation. Now carefully observe the underlined words of the *hadith*. You will see that when the superior *Janib* dates are exchanged with ordinary dates, there is the difference of double in one *sa$^c$s*, that is one *sa$^c$* of *Janib* dates are exchanged for two *sa$^c$s* of ordinary dates, but if you want to buy two *sa$^c$* of *Janib*, you will get it for only one and a half times more of ordinary dates, that is against only three *sa$^c$s*. In other words, there is a noticeable change in the rate of exchange from one *sa$^c$* to two *sa$^c$s* and the rate of exchange is not fixed. So, in order to avoid this, the Holy Prophet (*pbuh*) showed a method of buying and selling with coins, in which case there will be a fixed rate of exchange and there will be no possibility of a loss or deceit.

Even today in Indian villages female vegetable sellers go to houses to sell vegetables, but instead of cash they do business with grains and have a self-made rate of exchange for every kind of grain. Thus they cheat the naive women. For example, potatoes are sold sixteen kilograms for a *rupee*, barley ten kilograms and wheat eight kilograms. They will exchange a kilogram of potatoes for one and a quarter kilogram of barley or one kilogram of wheat or they will sell a quarter kilogram of *tarui* [a green vegetable] for half a kilogram of rice. Therefore, many wise men ask their women not to do this kind of shopping and tell them to sell the grain in excess of the annual requirement for cash and to buy things required with that money.

The Holy Prophet (*pbuh*) on this occasion taught a proper method of dealing according to the circumstances. To use this event in the argument about *riba* and that too in the *hand-to-hand* dealing is tantamount to توجيه القول بما لا يرضى به قائله (explaining a saying in a way which was not the intention of the speaker). When this same narration is narrated by another narrator on the authority of Abu Saʿid al-Khudari and Abu Hurayrah, instead of the singular 'don't do' لا تفعل, a plural 'don't do' لا تفعلوا is used. In other words, a particular instruction is generalised which converts a special order into a general order. The narrative narrates the latter part as follows:

ولكن مثلا .بمثل بيعوا بهذا واشتروا بثمنه هذا وكذلك الميزان (سنن الدارمي، القاهرة ، ١٩٧٨ ، ج ٢ ، ص ٢٥٨).

(But [exchange] equally, or sell it and with its price buy this, and that way is the balance).

Here in this case the narrator has himself added: مثلا بمثل (like for like) and narrated in his own words the method prescribed by the Holy Prophet (*pbuh*) after the word *aw* أو (Arabic for 'or').

## *(b)* The second narration

There is a similar narration by Abu Saʿid al-Khudari about another incident. The time of the incident is not evident from the actual narration but most probably it precedes the one in which the Holy Prophet (*pbuh*) had expressed his dislike regarding *Janib* dates because Bilal, knowing the Holy Prophet's dislike of the exchange of commodity-with-commodity and preference for sale and purchase with coins, would not have done that.

Let us suppose this incident occurred after the Khaybar dates incident, even then it probably happened around the same period and certainly precedes the revelation of the verses prohibiting *riba*. In order to appreciate the nature of the incident we present an authentic *hadith* narrated by Bilal, with its literal translation, free from all superfluities and explanatory annotations of the narrators:

كان عندي مُدٌّ للنبي صلى الله عليه وسلم فوجدت أطيب منه صاعا بصاعين منه فأتيت به النبي صلى الله عليه وسلم فقال : من أين لك هذا يا بلال؟ قلت: اشتريت صاعا بصاعين ، قال : رُدّه ورُدّ علينا تمرنا (سنن الدارمي ، القاهرة ، دار الفكر ، ١٩٧٨، ج ٢ ، ص ٢٥٧).

I had in the Prophet's [store] one *mudd*[10] [of dates]. I found better [dates] being sold at one *sa'* for two *sa's*, so I bought it [the better quality] and brought it to the Prophet. He asked, 'from where have you got it, Bilal?' I said I bought one *sa'* for two *sa's*. He said: 'return it and bring back to us our dates.'

This *hadith* ends there. The reason for that order is obvious: the Holy Prophet (*pbuh*) lived a very simple and frugal life, even the flour for his bread was not sieved, then how could he tolerate that just for the sake of gratification of the palate, two *sa's* of dates be exchanged with one *sa'* of better quality dates. Shah Waliullah *Muhaddith* Dihlawi, too, has mentioned the same reason for non-permissibility of *muratalah*. However, that order, too, was neither legislative nor had anything to do with *riba*.

The same incident is narrated in *al-Nasa'i* in the following words:

[أخبرنا نصر بن علي وإسماعيل بن مسعود واللفظ له عن خالد قال: حدثنا سعيد عن قتادة عن سعيد بن المسيب عن أبي سعيد الخدري] أن رسول الله صلى الله عليه وسلم أتى بتمر ريان وكان تمر رسول الله صلى الله عليه وسلم بعلا فيه يبس فقال: أنّى لكم هذا ؟ قالوا: ابتعناه صاعا بصاعين من تمرنا . فقال : "لا تفعل! فإن هذا لا يصح ، ولكن بع تمرك واشترِ من هذا حاجتك" (سنن النسائي بشرح السيوطي، كتاب البيوع ، باب بيع التمر بالتمر متفاضلا ، ط. دار الكتب العلمية، بيروت، ج ٧، ص ٢٧٢) .

Some juicy dates were presented to the Holy Prophet (*pbuh*). The Holy Prophet's dates from [his own orchard] at Al-'Ula were of the dry kind. He asked: 'where from have you got these dates?' People replied: we have bought one *sa'* of this with two *sa's* of our dates. He said: 'don't do it. It is not right. But sell your dates and buy of this according to your need.'

Now, look how much has been added to this *hadith* and the instructions given about the *Janib* dates of Khaybar have

---

[10] *Mudd* مُدّ is an Arabian measure equal to 1.33 pints (quarter of a *sa'*): Lane, *Arabic-English Lexicon*) (ed.).

been mixed with this one. However, this fell short of making up on one's own and did not dub this *muratalah* as *riba*. But in other narrations this *hadith* has been mixed up with the *hadith* saying التمر بالتمر ربا (dates for dates is *riba*) and, thereby, later narrators have mixed it up with the original narrative. Thus in one narrative, the following addition is found after the narration of this incident:

هذا الربا فردوه ثم بيعوا تمرنا واشتروا لنا من هذا.

This is *riba!* Return it, then sell our dates and buy for us from this.

In another narration this has been described as follows:

عن يحيى قال : سمعت عقبة بن العبد الغافر أنه سمع أبا سعيد الخدري رضي الله عنه قال : جاء بلال بتمر برنيّ فقال له النبي صلى الله عليه وسلم : من أين هذا ؟ قال بلال : كان عندنا تمر رديئ فبعت منه صاعين بصاع لنطعم النبي صلى الله عليه وسلم . فقال رسول الله صلى الله عليه وسلم عند ذلك : أوّه ! أوّه ! عين الربا، لا تفعل، ولكن إذا أردت أن تشتري فبع التمر ببيع آخر ثم اشتره (صحيح البخاري ، باب إذا باع الوكيل شيئا فاسدا فبيعه مردود، كتاب البيوع ، فتح الباري، ط. دار إحياء التراث العربي ، بيروت ، ١٤٠٢ هـ ، ج ٤ ، ص ٢٨٦).

.... Bilal brought *Barani* dates to the Holy Prophet (*pbuh*). The Prophet asked him from where are these? Bilal replied: We had inferior dates so I sold two *sa*ʿs for one *sa*ʿ for the consumption of the Prophet, *pbuh*. The Prophet said: Oh, oh, this is *riba* itself! Don't do so but whenever you want to buy, sell the dates for cash and then with that buy [those] dates.

Now this last part has been added to both *hadiths* here due to the misunderstanding of the narrators. It is certain that the verse prohibiting *riba* had not been revealed at the time of the conquest of Khaybar and it is also obvious that the Holy Prophet (*pbuh*) did not prohibit anything until and unless he received a revelation about it. Therefore, the dates' incident narrated by Bilal or Abu Saʿid al-Khudari or Abu Hurayrah cannot have any connection with *riba*. It is also certain that the people of Arabia did not regard this sort of hand-to-hand *muratalah*, in which the same or similar commodities were exchanged in greater or lesser quantity, as *riba*. Moreover, many authentic *ahadith* are available regarding the matter that hand-to-hand dealings have nothing to do with *riba*. So the utterance that this sort of dealing is *riba* cannot be that of the Holy Prophet (*pbuh*), because this will, in other words, mean that by that time *riba* dealing had already been proscribed. Thus it is certainly an addition by narrators. Other narrations of the same incident do not contain the words مثلا بمثل (equally) or هذا الربــا (this is *riba*). Thus the authentication of these narrations about *riba* by *fuqaha* is not correct.

### (c) Some instructions of the Holy Prophet (*pbuh*) about the conquest of Khaybar which have been wrongly used in the arguments regarding *riba*

Now we mention here some narratives as narrated by Fudalah ibn ᶜUbayd wherein the Holy Prophet (*pbuh*) had given some instructions to the *mujahidun* at Khaybar about selling silver and gold booty to the defeated Jews. These are the narrations used for strange arguments that hold selling silver and gold ware in equal weight of silver and gold as binding and any excess is held as '*riba*.'

But before quoting the actual narrations it seems necessary to draw the attention of readers to the fact that Khaybar was a centre of Jews who happened to be very rich. So when Khaybar was conquered Muslims got a lot of booty which included silver and gold ware. Muslim *mujahids* were used to a simple way of life, they did not know how to use those silver and gold wares, so they wanted to sell those wares for a trifle and get cash. Many people in fact sold at a price much lower than the actual value, that is, silver wares and ornaments weighing one *uqiyah*[11] were sold by them to Jews for two or three

---

[11] One *uqiyah* is equal to forty *dirhams* in weight (*Muntaha al-irab*).

pennies, whereas the weight of one *uqiyah* is several times more than two or three *dinars*[12].

When the Holy Prophet (*pbuh*) came to know that the *mujahids* were carelessly selling the booty, and that too to the conquered and deceitful Jews, he ordered that the God-given wealth should not be squandered like that, that at least they should check the weight of the things they sell and should not sell for a price less than that of its weight. This is the incident narrated by Fudalah ibn ʿUbayd in the following words:

عن فضالة بن عبيد قال : كنا مع رسـول الله صلى الله عليه وسلم يوم خيبر نبايع اليهود الوُقية الذهب بالدينارين والثلاثة ، فقال رسول الله صلى الله عليه وسلم : لا تبيعوا الذهب بالذهب إلا وزنـا بـوزن (صحيح مسلم ، كتاب المساقاة ، ج ٢ ، ص ١٢١٤).

We were with the Holy Prophet (*pbuh*) on the day of [the conquest of] Khaybar. We were selling Jews one *uqiyah* of gold for two and three *dinars*[13]. So the Holy Prophet (*pbuh*) said: do not sell gold for gold but in equal weight.

*Al-Nasa'i* records the following *hadith*, also narrated by Fudalah ibn ʿUbayd:

أخبرنا عمرو بن منصور قال ثنا محمد قال ثنا هُشَيم قـال أنبأنا الليـث بـن سعد عن خالد بن أبي عمران عن حنش الصنعاني عن فضالة بن عبيد قال : أصبت يوم خيبر قلادة فيها ذهب وخرز فـأردت أن أبيعها فذكـر ذلـك للنبي صلى الله عليه وسلم فقال : إفصل بعضَها من بعض ثم بعْها (صحيح النسائي ، كتاب البيوع، ط. دار الكتب العلمية، بيروت ، ج ٧ ، ص ٢٧٩) .

On the day of [the conquest of] Khaybar I got a studded golden necklace. I wanted to sell it. This was mentioned to the Holy Prophet (*pbuh*). He said: Separate them one from another and then sell them.

---

12   The word *'dinar'* is applicable to both coins of silver and gold. The ordinary weight of a *dinar* is 3.5 *masha* or one *mithqal* (*Muntaha al-irab* / Lane, *Arabic-English Lexicon*) (ed.).

13   One narration says بدينارين أو الثلاث (with two *dinars* or three) and some narrations have this piece: فبلغ ذلك رسول الله صلى الله عليه وسلم (so it reached the Prophet, *pbuh*).

## (d) The third narration

Then there is a third narration which says: On the same day Fudalah ibn ʿUbayd had purchased a necklace for twelve *dinars* which contained a jewel. Fudalah separated the jewel from the gold. He found that only the gold weighed more than twelve *dinars*. Probably after hearing the above-mentioned advice of the Holy Prophet (*pbuh*) Fudalah thought of enquiring about certain things which contain materials other than gold and how they could be weighed. The Holy Prophet replied: separate the gold and then weigh such things:

عن فضالة بن عبيد قال اشتريت يـوم خيبر قـلادة بإثني عشر دينارا فيها ذهب وخرز ففصلتها فوجدت فيها أكثر من إثني عشر دينارا فذكرتُ ذلك للنبي صلى الله عليه وسلم فقال : لا تباع حتى تفصل (صحيح مسلم، كتاب المساقاة : ٩٠ ، رقم الحديث ، ج ٢، ص ١٢١٣) .

Fudalah ibn ʿUbayd narrated that: on the day of Khaybar I bought a necklace for twelve *dinars*. It contained gold and a jewel. I separated [the jewel from the gold], I found in it [gold weighing] more than twelve *dinars*. I narrated this to the Holy Prophet (*pbuh*) who said: It should not be sold before it is separated.

Rationality suggests that all these three narrations are parts of the narration about the same incident. First of all the Holy Prophet got the information that the *mujahids* were throwing away the booty and were selling one *uqiyah* silver, *i.e.*, forty *dirham*[14] of silver in weight, for just two or three *dinars*. So the Prophet, upon whom be peace, stopped them from that wrong behaviour and said that they should sell things for a price equal at least to its weight, that is, at least the weight of gold or silver should be equal on both sides.

In this connection Fudalah, who had got a studded gold necklace as booty and probably twelve *dinars* were offered as its price, or he himself had bought it for twelve dinars and wanted to sell it, said: I have a gold necklace which is

---

[14] One *dirham* is equal to six *daniqs*, or $^1/_{12}$ of an *uqiyah*, or 3.12 grams (ed.).

jewel-studded and I want to sell it, so how should I do it because both gold and jewel are mingled, how could they be weighed? The Prophet, upon whom be peace, said: separate the jewel from the gold and then sell it. When Fudalah separated the jewel and weighed it, the gold itself was more than twelve *dinars* in weight. At that time the Prophet, upon whom be peace, said: separate the gold and then sell it.

This was the actual incident, of which you have read three different narrations. However, it is good that the narrators described them without any subtraction or addition.

## (e) The fourth narration

Now I quote a fourth narration of the same incident which has been narrated on the authority of this very same Fudalah ibn ʿUbayd but later narrators distorted various parts of the incident and narrated it, as they remembered, in a *third* way which altogether changed the actual incident and the meaning of the Holy Prophet's instruction. That narration is as follows:

سمعت فضالة بن عبيد الأنصاري يقول أُتي رسول الله صلى الله عليه وسلم وهو بخيبر بقلادة فيها خرز وذهب وهي من المغانم تباع، فأمر رسول الله صلى الله عليه وسلم بالذهب الذي في القلادة فنزع وحده، ثم قال لهم رسول الله صلى الله عليه وسلم: الذهب بالذهب وزنا بوزن (صحيح مسلم، كتاب المساقاة، رقم الحديث: ٨٩، ج ٢، ص ١٢١٣) .

I have heard Fudalah ibn ʿUbayd al-Ansari, saying that: on the day of the conquest of Khaybar, a jewel-studded necklace from the booty was brought to the Prophet, upon whom be peace, for sale. The Prophet, upon whom be peace, ordered that gold be separated [from the jewel] which was done. The Prophet then told them to sell the gold against gold in equal weight.

This narration does not mention that on the day of the conquest of Khaybar, the *mujahidun* were selling an *uqiyah* of gold for two or three *dinars* to the Jews and that due to this the Prophet, upon whom be peace, ordered them to sell

60

it by equal weight. This makes it difficult to understand the correct intention of the order.

Moreover, the incident itself has been distorted. The fact is that Fudalah himself wanted to sell the necklace and the Prophet, upon whom be peace, had given him instructions. It is not correct that the Prophet, upon whom be peace, himself sold the necklace in that manner. Even if this had been the case, how could it be that had someone offered the price of the gold in addition to the workmanship charges of the necklace and the price of the jewel, the Prophet, upon whom be peace, would have refused to accept it. It was not a *normal* commercial transaction, rather it was booty which was being sold by the *mujahidun* at a much lower price than its real value. The Prophet stopped this reckless business and said that the price fetched should be at least equal to the actual price of the gold, that it should not be sold for a lower price. But where is the prohibition for selling it at a higher price?

The object of that order was only that Muslims should not suffer losses in selling the booty. This is not the opinion of this humble person, ʿ*Allamah* Al-Tahawi, a *muhaddith* of a very high stature and one of the pillars of the Hanafi *fiqh*, says that the reason for this instruction was that لأن لا يُغبن المسلمون في بيوعهم (so that Muslims should not be cheated in their trading).

Even today the normal practice all over the world is that if someone buys silver or gold ware, such as ornaments or *attardan*, he will have to pay the workmanship charges in addition to the cost of gold and silver. But if he needs to sell the very same ornament and the buyer is not interested in the workmanship he will get a price equal to the value of silver and gold. A buyer who does not require the workmanship, will not pay the additional charges.

However, when you read these *ahadith* repeatedly, you will fail to find the word '*riba*' anywhere. What is the sense in using these *ahadith* in the argument for *riba*? Do remember that until that time the *ayah* on the prohibition of *riba* had not been revealed and this is the reason why the *muhaddithun*, like Ibn Majah and Imam al-Bukhari, have narrated these *ahadith* under the chapters of *Bayʿ Sarf* and

*Bay' Muratalah*. But some people somehow regard these narrations as related to *riba* and make a peculiar inference of *Fiqh* that if articles made of silver and gold are bought against silver and gold coins then they should be equal in weight and the workmanship charges should not be given because this will amount to eating *riba*! God bless *Imam* Ibn Taymiyah who raised his voice against this.

Now, we are going to quote a series of narratives regarding a *khutbah* of Abu 'Ubadah ibn al-Samit on a similar incident.

There was a *jihad* during the reign of *Amirul Mu'minin* Mu'awiyah. The spoils of war included silver and gold ware. People were buying and selling those things among themselves. 'Ubadah had heard the Holy Prophet say: لا تبيعوا الذهب بالذهب إلا سواءا بسواء (do not sell gold with gold except equally). He had also heard instructions about face-to-face transactions of *bay' sarf* (exchange). So he collected these individual and different instructions and gave a *khutbah* which is as follows according to the narration of Muslim ibn Yasar on the authority of Abu al-Ash'ath:

أيها الناس إنكم قد أحدثتم بيوعا لا أدري ما هي ! ألا إن الذهب بالذهب وزنا بوزن تبرها وعينها، وإن الفضة بالفضة وزنا بوزن تبرها وعينها، ولا بأس ببيع الفضة بالذهب يدا بيد والفضة أكثرهما، ولا تصلح النسيئة. ألا إن البر بالبر والشعير بالشعير مدّا بمدّ ، حتى ذكر الملح مدا بمد فمن زاد أو استزاد فقد أربى (سنن النسائي، كتاب البيوع ، ج ٧، ص ٢٧٨) .

People! you have innovated new sorts of buying and selling which I do not understand. Beware! Gold, both nuggets and coins, is to be sold against gold, weight for weight. Silver, both nuggets and coins, is to be sold against silver, weight for weight. It is all right to sell silver against gold while silver is greater in quantity. Credit [advance or credit transaction] is not all right. Wheat is to be sold against wheat, barley against barley, weight for weight. He went on until he mentioned salt to be sold weight for weight [and added] whoever increased or sought increase commits *riba*.

Now see: it is quite clear from the whole narration that this is a personal opinion of Abu ᶜUbadah. Nowhere has he said that this is the Prophet's *(pbuh)* order. The same incident about the same ᶜUbadah by the same Abul Ash'ath as narrated by Ayyub on the authority of Abu Qulaba has been narrated in the following words by *Imam* Muslim in his *Sahih*. The narrator is ᶜUbaydullah.

### *(f)* ᶜUbaydullah's narration

... ينهـى [رسـول الله صلى الله عليـه وسلم] عن بيـع الذهـب بالذهب والفضة بالفضة والبر بالبر والشعير بالشعير والتمر بـالتمر والملح بالملح إلا سواءا بسواء عينا بعين ، فمن زاد أو ازداد فقد أربى

(صحيح مسلم، كتاب المساقاة، رقم الحديث ٨٠ ، ج ٢، ص ١٢١٠).

The Prophet, upon whom be peace, prohibits the selling of gold with gold, silver with silver, wheat with wheat, barley with barley, dates with dates, salt with salt, except equally, kind for kind. <u>So whoever increased or sought an increase committed *riba*</u>.

From this, it seems clear that the underlined portion is ᶜUbadah's own inference, while in the foregoing part ᶜUbadah, in his own words, tried to state the meaning of the Prophet's *(pbuh)* saying.

But the second narration, which is in *al-Nasa'i* (فمن زاد واز داد فقد أربى), indicates that the inference is that of later narrators. But this narration creates the misunderstanding that the remaining portion of the narration, instead of being part of the *khutbah* of Abu ᶜUbadah, is the saying of the Holy Prophet *(pbuh)*:

أخبرنا محمد بن المثنى ويعقوب بن إبراهيم، قـالا : حدثنا عمرو بن عاصم، قال : حدثنا همام ، قال : حدثنا قتادة عن أبي الخليل عـن مسلم المكي عن أبي الأشعث الصنعاني عن عبادة بن الصامت قـال: قال رسول الله صلى الله عليه وسلم : الذهب بـالذهب تـبره وعينه وزنا بوزن ، والفضة بالفضة تبره وعينه وزنا بوزن ، والملح بالملح ،

والتمر بالتمر ، والبر بالبر ، والشعير بالشعير ، سواءا بسواء مثلا
بمثل، فمن زاد أو ازداد فقد أربى، واللفظ لمحمد، لم يذكر يعقوب:
والشعير بالشعير (صحيح النسائي، كتاب البيوع ، باب بيع الشعير بالشعير،
ج ٧، ص٢٧٦ – ٢٧٧) .

The Prophet, upon whom be peace, said, gold [is sold] against gold weight for weight, both nuggets and coins, silver [is sold] against silver, weight for weight, both nuggets and coins. And salt against salt, dates against dates, wheat against wheat, barley against barley, equal for equal, and kind for kind. Whoever, increased or sought an increase, committed *riba*.

However, when *Amirul Mu'minin* Muᶜawiyah heard about the *khutbah* of Abu ᶜUbadah, he himself delivered a *khutbah* and said that there was no such saying of the Prophet (*pbuh*) which could be interpreted as Abu ᶜUbadah had deduced. The following is the remaining portion of this narration that Muᶜawiyah said in his *khutbah*:

ألا ما بال رجال يتحدثون عن رسول الله صلى الله عليه وسلم
أحاديث؛ قد كنا نشهده ونصحبه فلم نسمعها منه (صحيح مسلم،
كتاب المساقاة ٨٠ ، رقم الحديث ، ج ٢ ، ص ١٢١٠ ؛ وبكلمات متقاربة فى
صحيح النسائي ، كتاب البيوع ، ج ٧ ، ص ٢٧٦).

What has happened to people that they attribute such sayings to the Holy Prophet (*pbuh*). We witnessed him and used to accompany him but we never heard such things from him.

When ᶜUbadah heard this, he repeated what he had uttered earlier and said: 'We will keep narrating the Prophet's sayings although Muᶜawiyah may dislike it.'

There is no doubt that ᶜUbadah disliked the objection of Muᶜawiyah because, although ᶜUbadah had erred in understanding the saying of the Prophet and in his inferences from it, his error was based on good intention. Muᶜawiyah's objection was based on ᶜUbadah's interpretation, so he, too, was right in the stand he took.

Now let us see if ᶜUbadah narrated in the Prophet's words also or not? One narration has it that ᶜUbadah repeated what he had said earlier (فأعاد القصة). But what *Musnad Ahmad* has mentioned as narrated by Hakim ibn Jabir includes the following words:

عن عبادة بن الصامت قال : سمعت رسولَ الله صلى الله عليه وسلم
يقول : الذهب بالذهب ، والفضة بالفضة ، مثلاً بمثل ، حتى خص
الملح، فقال معاوية : إن هذا لا يقول شيئا ، فقال عبادة : لا أبالي
أن لا أكون بأرض يكون فيها معاوية ، أشهد أني سمعت رسول الله
صلى الله عليه وسلم يقول ذلك (مسند أحمد بن حنبل ، ج ٥ ، ص
٣١٩).

It is narrated by ᶜUbadah ibn al-Samit, he said: I heard the Holy Prophet (*pbuh*), saying 'gold with gold, silver with silver, in equal weight;' [he went on] until he mentioned salt. So Muᶜawiyah said: 'this does not say anything.' Upon this ᶜUbadah said: 'I don't care not to live in Muᶜawiyah's country. I witness that I heard the Prophet saying it.'

The same narration by Hakim ibn Jabir is mentioned in *al-Nasa'i* in the following words:

أخبرني هارون بن عبدالله، قال : حدثنا أبو أسامة، قال : قال
إسماعيل : حدثنا حكيم بن جابر ح وأنبأنا يعقوب بن إبراهيم، قال:
حدثنا يحيى عن إسماعيل، حدثنا : حكيم بن جابر عن عبادة بن
الصامت، قال: سمعت رسول الله صلى الله عليه وسلم يقول :
الذهب بالكفة بالكفة – ولم يذكر يعقوب الكفة بالكفة – فقال
معاوية: إن هذا لا يقول شيئا . قال عبادة : إني والله ما أبالي أن لا
أكون بأرض يكون بها معاوية . إني أشهد أني سمعت رسول الله
صلى الله عليه وسلم يقول ذلك (صحيح النسائي، كتاب البيوع ، ج ٧،
ص ٢٧٧ – ٢٧٨).

ᶜUbadah ibn al-Samit said: I heard the Holy Prophet (*pbuh*) saying: gold for gold, scale for scale — Yaᶜqub [one of the two narrators] did not mention the words 'scale for scale'— . [Upon hearing this] Muᶜawiyah said: This does not say anything. ᶜUbadah said: By God, I don't care if I would

**65**

not live in Mu<sup>c</sup>awiyah's country. I witness that I heard the Holy Prophet (pbuh) saying this.

Just imagine: how could the Prophet's words, narrated by <sup>c</sup>Ubadah after the objection of Mu<sup>c</sup>awiyah, be interpreted as what <sup>c</sup>Ubadah inferred in his *khutbah*? This is why after hearing the wording of the narration, Mu<sup>c</sup>awiyah said what every rational person would say, that is: this narration does not say anything.

See how one thing becomes completely another. Later narrators added their inferences and narrated the incident in their own words. Thus gradually it took the shape of a mixture which was not stated by the Holy Prophet (pbuh), neither was it stated by <sup>c</sup>Ubadah nor by those who narrated it on the authority of <sup>c</sup>Ubadah, that is, Abu al-Ash<sup>c</sup>ath, Hakim ibn Jabir and <sup>c</sup>Abdallah ibn <sup>c</sup>Ubayd. Some of the additions are those of Abu Qulaba, Khalid al-Hadda' and Abu Sufyan and some are by Muhammad ibn Sirin and Waki<sup>c</sup> and other later narrators. Thus Isma<sup>c</sup>il ibn Mas<sup>c</sup>ud narrates it in the following words only:

قال عبادة : نهى رسول الله صلى الله عليه وسلم أن نبيع الذهـب بالذهب والورق بالورق والبر بالـبر والشعير بالشعير والتمـر بـالتمر (النسائي، كتاب البيوع ، ج ٧ ، ص ٢٧٥).

<sup>c</sup>Ubadah said: the Prophet of Allah, upon whom be peace, prohibited that we sell gold for gold, silver for silver, wheat for wheat, barley for barley, and dates for dates.

Muhammad ibn Sirin narrated the same with many additions but he has made these additions rather carefully and stated that <sup>c</sup>Abdallah ibn <sup>c</sup>Ubayd and Muslim ibn Yasar both have narrated it on the authority of <sup>c</sup>Ubadah ibn al-Samit, although Muslim ibn Yasar's direct narration from <sup>c</sup>Ubadah is not established. Ibn Sirin has narrated from both of them at the same time and wherever he had any doubt he said that it was narrated by one of them but without specifying the name. Following is Ibn Sirin's narration:

حدثني مسلم بن يسار وعبـدالله بن عُبيـد ، وقد كـان يدعى ابن هرمز، قال: جمع المنزل بين عبادة بن الصامت وبين معاوية . حدثهم عبادة قال: نهانا رسول الله صلى الله عليه وسلم عـن بيـع الذهـب

66

بالذهب والفضة بالفضة والتمر بالتمر والبر بالبر والشعير بالشعير –
وقال أحدهما : والملح بالملح ولم يقله الآخر – إلا سواءا بسواء
ومثلا بمثل. قال أحدهما : من زاد أو ازداد فقد أربى ولم يقله الآخر
(صحيح النسائي، كتاب البيوع، ج ٧، ص ٢٧٥) .

Muslim ibn Yasar and ᶜAbdallah ibn ᶜUbayd, who was
called 'Ibn Hurmuz,' narrated to me that ᶜUbadah ibn
al-Samit and Muᶜawiyah met once. ᶜUbadah narrated to
them: 'The Prophet, upon whom be peace, forbade us to
sell gold for gold, silver for silver, dates for dates, wheat for
wheat, barley for barley — one of them [the two narrators]
said: 'and salt for salt' while the other did not say it —
except quantity for quantity and kind for kind. One of
them said: whoever increased or sought an increase
committed *riba* — the other [narrator] did not say it.

Now the following points are to be considered in this
*hadith*:

(*a*) ᶜAbdallah ibn ᶜUbayd was also called 'Ibn Hurmuz'
which indicates that he was of Persian origin and it is
likely that he could not properly comprehend
ᶜUbadah's view point. And although Muslim ibn Yasar
was an Arab, he had not heard it directly from
ᶜUbadah, so whatever he heard was from someone else.

(*b*) ᶜUbadah also does not say that the Holy Prophet
(*pbuh*) said so (قال رسول الله صلى الله عليه وسلم) but says that
the Holy Prophet (*pbuh*) 'forbade' us (نهانا رسول الله صلى
الله عليه وسلم). This indicates that ᶜUbadah has in his own
words stated the Prophet's meaning as he understood
it. Moreover, regarding the actual point of difference,
that is: (من زاد أو استزاد فقد أربى) ('whoever increased or
sought an increase committed *riba*'), Muhammad ibn
Sirin says that out of two narrators one has not stated it
and does not tell us who did not state it.

When this narration is stated by Wakiᶜ, more
additions creep into it, to the extent that instead of '[the
Holy Prophet (*pbuh*)] forbade us نهانا', the new
wording says: 'the Prophet, upon whom be peace, said'
(قال رسول الله صلى الله عليه وسلم) which creates the

impression that these are the very words of the Holy Prophet (*pbuh*) himself; and secondly, the piece: فإذا اختلفت الأصناف فبيعوا كيف شئتم (if the kinds are different then trade as you like), which is Waki's own *fiqhi* inference, becomes a part of the narration. Now, let us re-consider the above-mentioned narration of *al-Nasa'i*:

أخبرنا محمد بن المثنى ويعقوب بن إبراهيم، قالا : حدثنا عمرو بـن عاصم، قال : حدثنا همام ، قال : حدثنا قتادة عن أبي الخليل عن مسلم المكي عن أبي الأشعث الصنعاني عـن عبادة بن الصامت قال: قال رسول الله صلى الله عليه وسلم : الذهب بالذهب تـبره وعينه وزنا بوزن ، والفضة بالفضة تبره وعينه وزنا بوزن ، والملـح بالملح ، والتمـر بـالتمر ، والبـر بالبر ، والشـعير بالشعير ، سواءا بسواء مثلا بمثل، فمن زاد أو ازداد فقـد أربـى، واللفظ لمحمد، لم يذكر يعقوب: والشعير بالشعير (صحيح النسائي، كتـاب البيـوع ، بـاب بيع الشعير بالشعير، ج ٧، ص٢٧٦ – ٢٧٧) .

The Prophet, upon whom be peace, said, gold is [sold] against gold, weight for weight, both nuggets and coins, silver is [sold] against silver, weight for weight, both nuggets and coins. And salt against salt, dates against dates, wheat against wheat, barley against barley, equal for equal, and kind for kind [equally]. Whoever, increased or sought an increase committed *riba*.

It is Muhammad ibn al-Muthanna who has added the words 'Whoever, increased or sought an increase committed *riba*.' Moreover, by beginning ʿUbadah's *khutbah* with the words 'the Holy Prophet said,' he changed the inference of a *sahabi* into a saying of the Holy Prophet himself.

## 12.
## Instructions about *muratalah* and *bay<sup>c</sup> sarf* mixed up with *riba*

However, after thoroughly considering the above-mentioned *ahadith*, one thing becomes abundantly clear that the Prophet, upon whom be peace, had given some instructions about *muratalah* (barter) in connection with certain actual situations with the sole intention that commodities and coins should not be mutually exchanged and if such an exchange does take place none of the parties suffers a loss. These narrations have nothing to do with the rule about *riba*, neither has the Prophet, upon whom be peace, considered any increase in such cases as '*riba*.' Even by the time these instructions were issued, that is by the time of the conquest of Khaybar, the verse prohibiting *riba* had not been revealed.

This also indicates that these instructions are not legislative orders. Had *muratalah* or *bay<sup>c</sup> sarf* been non-permissible then, at the time of the revelation of the Qur'anic verses prohibiting *riba*, both *bay<sup>c</sup> sarf* and *bay<sup>c</sup> muratalah* would have also been simultaneously prohibited – that is, the cases wherein commodity is exchanged with commodity with an increase in hand-to-hand dealings. The mistakes committed by some *fuqaha*, may Allah bless them, is due to the fact that after the passing away of the Prophet (*pbuh*) some narrators of *ahadith* due to doubts mixed the instructions about *riba* with the instructions about *muratalah* and *bay<sup>c</sup> sarf* and deduced wrong instructions as a result. Later these were included as the Prophet's (*pbuh*) sayings by later narrators. Thus when *Fuqaha* based their inferences on those *ahadith* the mistake was inevitable.

In this connection it seems necessary to mention different instructions about *bay<sup>c</sup> sarf* and *muratalah* in different *ahadith*. But first let us mention some related matters by way of introduction.

69

## 13.

# Instructions about mutual exchange
# of coins have no connection with *riba*

It is common knowledge that there was no proper government in pre-Islam Arabia and in the early period of the Prophethood, neither was there an official currency. The Arabs' only source of livelihood, in addition to cattle-raising and piracy, was trade with bordering countries like Yemen, Iraq, Persia, Egypt and Abyssinia. Those countries had different governments and all of them had separate currencies of silver or gold. The weight of those coins were different in every country. But the Arabs called every silver coin 'dirham' whatever be its weight. Similarly every gold coin of whatever weight was called 'dinar'.[15] Sometimes big silver coins were also called *dinar*. These coins also varied according to their standards. Some coins had good quality silver while some others had bad silver, some had pure gold and some others had impure gold. It also happened that a trader returning from Abyssinia this year wanted to take his merchandise to Persia next year. Another one has returned from Persia and intends to go to Abyssinia. Sometimes they needed coins to buy their merchandise. A trader borrowed from another trader to buy merchandise and returned the same number of coins when he came back. Thus there was the need for the mutual exchange of coins. This was termed by Arabs as *bay' sarf* that is currency dealing. It is said in Arabic dictionaries:

إذا بيع الذهب بالذهب أو الفضة بالفضة سمي "مراطلة" وإذا بيع الذهب بالفضة سمي "صرفا".

When gold is sold for gold and silver for silver, it is called *Muratalah* and when gold is sold for silver it is called *sarf*.

In most cases one or the other partner would be a loser in the exchange of coins of different weights and qualities. For

---

[15] The Arab/Islamic *dinar* is equal to one *mithqal* in weight, i.e., one and three sevenths of a *dirham*. One *mithqal* is equal to 4.68 grams (ed.).

example, one *dinar* is exchanged for one *dinar* but the gold of one is pure and of more weight and the gold of the other is impure and less in weight and the one who has better coin, is in need of exchange. In this case if he exchanges *dinar* for *dinar* he is going to be a loser. Similarly if one *dinar* is exchanged for two *dinars* but the difference in the value is only one and a half then the person having a *dinar* of lesser value will be a loser and so on.

Suppose I took some Abyssinian *dinars* from you and went to Persia. I brought the same number of coins from there and returned them to you but they are of lesser value. This raises a controversy. You say that your *dinars* were of greater value, I say that my *dinars* are better. The *dinars* you had given, by now have reached God knows where. It is difficult to compare them now.[16]

---

[16] With regard to the exchange of currencies, one thing is to be noted that if someone is not doing currency exchange as a profession his charging for the exchange is looked down upon with disapproval. For example, I am a lawyer and you are a professor. I have currency notes and you need currency notes which you want to exchange with silver *rupees*. In such circumstances, if I charge an amount for exchanging the currency notes, it is certainly not *riba* but still it is an absurd act. The cash I received in exchange for the currency notes is of the same monetary value. I did not make any extra effort in supplying the currency notes, so I should not get any extra amount as charges for the exchange. But if a currency exchanger, in view of people's needs, has opened up shop and supplies various currencies and spends his time and money for this business, why should he not charge for his labour? It is like this: if a rich person by chance arrives at the house of another rich person at the meal time and eats some bread, will the person with the bread charge a price for the bread? But will you not pay to the restaurateur who is in this very business? There was another problem in Arabia that there were no professional money exchangers.

## 14.
# Instructions of the Prophet about *bay<sup>c</sup> sarf*

These were the circumstances because of which the Holy Prophet (*pbuh*) gave some instructions about *bay<sup>c</sup> sarf* on different occasions. About *bay<sup>c</sup> muratalah*, the Prophet, upon whom be peace, directed not to exchange similar commodities with one another. Instead, he instructed: sell your commodity for cash and buy other commodity with that cash. Similarly he gave two instructions about *bay<sup>c</sup> sarf*:

1. Parties should deal hand-to-hand, that is, parties intending to exchange currencies should be present at the time of the deal so that every party could inspect the quantity and quality of the other's commodity and satisfy himself. It should not happen that I take some coins from you today and make a promise about the coins I have to give you tomorrow, because in that case there is the possibility of dishonesty or misunderstanding.

2. The second instruction about *bay<sup>c</sup> sarf* was that coins should be exchanged *equally* according to their value, that is, every party to the exchange should get equal value according to both the weight and quality. So in addition to inspecting the purity and impurity, weight will also have to be considered in order to fix the quantity. These are the narrations about *bay<sup>c</sup> sarf* and most of them are narrated by Abu Sa<sup>c</sup>id al-Khudari.

## 15.
## Some narrations about *bay<sup>c</sup> sarf*

### (a) Abu Sa<sup>c</sup>id al-Khudari's narrative

عن أبي سعيد الخدري أن رسول الله صلى الله عليه وسلم قال: لا
تبيعوا الذهب بالذهب إلا مثلا بمثل ولا تشِفوا بعضها على بعض
ولاتبيعوا الورق بالورق إلا مثلا بمثل ولا تشِفوا بعضها على بعض
ولا تبيعوا منها غائبا بناجز (صحيح البخاري، كتاب البيوع، باب بيع
الفضة بالفضة، فتح الباري، ج ٤، ص ٣٠٢) .

Abu Sa<sup>c</sup>id al-Khudari narrates that the Holy Prophet
(*pbuh*) said: Do not exchange gold with gold except kind
for kind, and do not increase one on the other, and do not
exchange silver with silver except kind for kind [equally],
and do not increase one against the other, and do not
exchange what is present with what is not.

Another narration, also by Abu Sa<sup>c</sup>id al-Khudari, is similar
in meaning but in different words:

لا تبيعوا الذهب بالذهب ولا الورق بالورق إلا وزنا بوزن ، مثلا
بمثل، سواء بسواء .

Do not sell gold for gold or silver for silver except weight
for weight, kind for kind, equal for equal.

This narration does not include the last portion of the
forgoing *hadith*, that is ولا تبيعوا منها غائبا بناجز (and do not
exchange what is present with what is not). But in some
other *ahadith*, يدا بيد (hand-to-hand) is mentioned instead.
Another thing worth considering in this narration is that
it contains three groups of words: وزنا بوزن (weight for
weight), مثلا بمثل (kind for kind) and سواء بسواء (equal for
equal). But some narrations have only مثلا بمثل (kind for
kind) and some have only سواء بسواء (equal for equal). And in
some instead of وزنا بوزن (weight for weight) we find الكفة
بالكفة (scale for scale). And in some, as in the above

73

mentioned narration, there is ولا تَشِفُّوا بعضها على بعض (and do not increase one against the other).

Now we have to see if in this narration all the three groups of words (weight for weight/kind for kind/equal for equal) are completely synonymous or have different meanings? If they are synonymous, what do they mean? Some *fuqaha*, who consider them as synonymous, believe that they mean equal quantity, that is, silver should be equal in weight to silver and gold should be equal in weight to gold.

Because of this misunderstanding, some narrators of *ahadith* and some *fuqaha* have said that جيدها ورديّنها سواء (its good and inferior qualities are equal). But this is the inference of narrators or respected *fuqaha*. The intent of the Prophet's (*pbuh*) saying is completely contrary to it and the reason is obvious: why should the Holy Prophet (*pbuh*) use three synonymous groups of words unnecessarily? If it is said that synonymous words were used in this *hadith* only for the sake of emphasis, I would submit that in the first *hadith* after having said مثلا بمثل (kind for kind), there is a word of conjunction and then there is a negative sentence. So if مثلا بمثل (kind for kind) meant that gold or silver should be in equal weight on both sides then where was the need to add these words ولا تَشِفُّوا بعضها على بعض *i.e.*, do not increase one against the other. Thus it is clear that just as 'weight for weight/kind for kind/equal for equal' are literally different in meaning, they have been used to convey different meanings. So مثلا بمثل (kind for kind) means that the two commodities must be equal in quality, بوزن وزنا (weight for weight) means that they should be equal in weight.

Now it is likely that shortage or excess in quality is offset by the shortage or excess in quantity, that is, in the case of inequality of quality and quantity, the two variables of quality and quantity together make up for equality on both sides which is the objective intent of the instruction. This is the reason why a comprehensive word سواء بسواء (equal for equal) has been used in most of the narratives as it covers both meanings. That is why in most narrations only سواء بسواء (equal for equal) has been considered as sufficient. So the words 'its good and inferior qualities are equal,' as mentioned in some narrations, are not only against reason and rationally wrong, it is a wrong narration as well and it is totally against the intent of the saying of the Holy Prophet (pbuh). This part has been added by the narrator who made this addition while narrating the meaning of the hadith.

## (b) Abu Hurayrah's narrative

There is a narration narrated by Abu Hurayrah in *Muslim* and *al-Nasa'i* which says that exchange of barley for barley and wheat with wheat with an increase is permissible when the colours are different.[17] Similarly, there is the following narration in *Ibn Majah*:

الدرهم بالدرهم والدينار بالدينار ولا فضل بينهما إلا وزنا (ابن ماجة، كتاب التجارات، رقم الحديث ٢٢٥٦ ، ج ٢، ص ٧٥٨) .

> *Dirham* for *dirham* and *dinar* for *dinar,* and there should not be any increase in their exchange except in case of weight [*i.e.,* only if the weight of one coin is greater than the other].

It is noteworthy here that all these *ahadith*, that mention more rational methods of sale and purchase than *muratalah* (barter), common among Arabs, or those that advise keeping in mind weight and quality to ensure equality between transacting parties and make it compulsory for the parties to be present at the time of exchange, these *ahadith* generally begin with the negative form لا تبيعوا (do not sell) and the word *riba* does not occur therein anywhere. In some narrations, only the style of statement is different. But such narrations are those that do not quote the exact wording of the Prophet's saying but paraphrase it in the narrator's own words, *i.e.,* they contain whatever a

---

[17] *Sahih Muslim*, Kitab al-masaqath, Bab al-sarf wa bay' al-dahab bi'l-wariq naqdan, *hadith* No. 83/1588, p. 1211; *Al-Nasa'i*, Kitab al-buyu', bab bay' al-tamr bi'l-tamr, vol. 7, pp. 273f (ed.).

companion understood of a certain instruction of the Prophet (*pbuh*) or expressed an opinion after the Prophet's death about a certain dealing or event taking place at the time, and, for authenticating his opinion, he narrated some sayings of the Holy Prophet (*pbuh*) in his own words, and the style of his statement is such that the inference of the narrator or a companion get intermingled with the Prophet's saying. Later opinions of narrators down the chain get mixed up further and completely distort the original structure of the Prophet's saying. This has been dealt with in detail while discussing the narration of the *khutbah* of ʿUbadah.

The narrations relating to *bayʿ muratalah* and *bayʿ sarf*, whose actual occurrence in point of time are not known, met the same fate. Thus the above-mentioned narration has been narrated by various narrators on the authority of Abu Saʿid al-Khudari and all their texts are different. Most narrations do not contain the word '*riba*' at all; some have the word *riba* and one of them has this piece: فإني أخاف عليكم الربا (I am afraid that you may commit *riba*). This sentence cannot be that of the Holy Prophet (*pbuh*) because this means that by that time the verses dealing with the prohibition of *riba* had already been revealed. Secondly, why should the Holy Prophet (*pbuh*) be afraid? He (*pbuh*) could have simply said that it was *riba*. If the Holy Prophet (*pbuh*) had doubts about that dealing being *riba* then why should our doubts be held as wrong? In fact, these words are those of Abu Saʿid al-Khudari himself and through the first-person narration he expresses his own fear, or later narrators have added these words.[18]

---

[18] The part أخاف عليكم الربا (I am afraid that you may commit *riba*) has been changed in other narrations to: فمن زاد أو ازداد فقد أربى (whoever increases or seeks an increase commits *riba*). It may also be noted that its first narrator is that very same Abu Saʿid al-Khudari. So it is quite likely that the matter about the dates of Khaybar got mixed up with the Khaybar booty story and with the addition by later narrators it took this form of narration.

Now we want to mention some other similar narrations which have nothing to do with *riba* but some people use them for authenticating their definition of *riba*:

حدثنا عبدالرحمن بن أبي بكرة عن أبيه قال : نهى رسول الله صلى الله عليه وسلم عن بيع الفضة بالفضة والذهب بالذهب إلا سواءا بسواء . وأمرنا أن نشتري الفضة بالذهب كيف شئنا، ونشتري الذهب بالفضة كيف شئنا . فسأله رجل فقال : يدا بيد (صحيح مسلم، كتاب المساقاة، رقم الحديث ٨٨ ، ج ٢ ، ص ١٢١٣).

It is narrated through ʿAbd al-Rahman ibn Abi Bakrah[19] on the authority of his father that the Holy Prophet (*pbuh*) forbade the exchange of silver with silver and of gold with gold except equally. And he ordered us to exchange gold with silver and silver with gold in whatever way we like. A person asked him [a question to which] he said: hand-to-hand.

Let us probe this narration. First of all, this narration is not a direct quote of the Prophet's words but a paraphrase and interpretation by the narrator. Probably it is a brief summary of the narrations already mentioned above. The Holy Prophet's (*pbuh*) words, to the extent possible, have been used in those *ahadith*. But instead of the words لا تبيعوا (do not sell), it uses the word نهى ([The Prophet] forbade). And instead of لا تبيعوا منها غائبا بناجز (and do not exchange what is present with what is not), it uses يدا بيد (hand-to-hand), and between these two parts it has mentioned the narrator's own inference from وأمرنا.... (and he ordered us...) to كيف شئنا (whatever way we like). See for yourself that in the mutual exchange of silver and gold, difference of quantity is necessary, may it be in cash or on credit, then what is the relationship of يدا بيد (hand-to-hand) with this? Does this mean that if the exchange is not hand-to-hand then silver will have to be exchanged with gold in equal quantity?.. The reality seems to be that in this narration a misunderstanding has been caused by ʿUbadah ibn al-

---

[19] Abu Bakrah is a person other than Abu Bakr al-Siddiq.

Samit's narration as quoted by Waki[c] which is in the following words:

عن عبادة بن الصامت قال : قال رسول الله صلى الله عليه وسلم:
الذهب بالذهب والفضة بالفضة والبر بالبر والشعير بالشعير والتمر
بالتمر والملح بالملح ، مثلاً بمثل ، سواءاً بسواء ، يداً بيد ، فإذا
اختلفت هذه الأصناف فبيعوا كيف شئتم إذا كان يداً بيد (صحيح
مسلم، كتاب المساقاة ، رقم الحديث ٨١ ، ج ٢، ص ١٢١١).

[c]Ubadah ibn al-Samit said that the Prophet of Allah, upon whom be peace, said: [exchange] <u>gold for gold, silver for silver, wheat for wheat, barley for barley, dates for dates and salt for salt, kind for kind, like for like and hand-to-hand.</u> If these commodities are different then exchange as you like if it is hand-to-hand.

Probably this *hadith* too is one from the chain of narrations which [c]Ubadah, inspired by the event of Khaybar, narrated in his own words or it may be a piece from his above-mentioned *khutbah*.

In any case, [c]Ubadah has, in this *hadith*, narrated the Holy Prophet's (*pbuh*) instructions, given on various occasions, in his own [[c]Ubadah's] words which are underlined. Words occurring after the underlined portion are those of Abu [c]Ubadah or the inferences of later narrators and this very addition occurs in the narration by Abu Bakra with changed wording and the words يداً بيد (hand-to-hand), which occur here twice, are excluded from the first part of the narration by Abu Bakra where, in fact, they should have been. However, both of these narrations indicate only this much: that whether it is an exchange of commodity with commodity or exchange of cash with cash, in both cases there should be equality of value and the parties should witness the exchanged goods at the time of transaction and take possession of it. These *ahadith* have nothing to do with *riba*.

Now let us scrutinize another narration whose narrator is *Amirul Mu'minin* [c]Umar ibn al-Khattab whose greatness

78

cannot be doubted by any faithful. Following is the wording of his narration:

عن مالك بن أوس بن الحدثان أنه قال : أقبلت أقول : مَن يصطرف الدراهم ؟ فقال طلحة بن عبدالله – وهو عند عمر بن الخطاب – : أرنا ذهبَك ثم آتنا إذا جاء خادمنا نعطيك ورقـك . فقـال عمـر بـن الخطاب : كلا ! والله لتعطينّه ورقه أو لتردنّ إليه ذهبه فإن رسـول الله صلى الله عليه وسلم قال : الورق بالذهب ربا إلا هـاء وهـاء ، والبر بالبر ربا إلا هاء وهـاء، والشعير بالشعير ربـا إلا هـاء وهـاء ، والتمر بالتمر ربا إلا هاء وهاء (**صحيح مسلم**، كتاب المساقاة، رقم الحديث ٧٩ ، ج ٢ ، ص ١٢٠٩) .

Malik ibn Aws ibn al-Hadathan said that he came asking: who exchanges *dirhams*? Talha ibn ᶜAbdallah said, while sitting by the side of ᶜUmar, 'show me your gold then come to us when our servant comes, we will give you silver coins.' So ᶜUmar said, 'Never! by God, either you give him the silver [now] or return his gold because the Prophet (*pbuh*) had said that silver for gold was *riba* except when [the exchange] is hand-to-hand and barley with barley is *riba* except when [the exchange] is hand-to-hand and dates with dates is *riba* except when [the exchange] is hand-to-hand.'

I would submit that in this narration the wordings after 'because the Prophet (*pbuh*) had said' cannot be those of ᶜUmar. These are the words of later narrators because ᶜUmar himself has stated that the Prophet passed away before interpreting the verse about *riba*. Then how can the same ᶜUmar attribute such a detailed definition of *riba* to the Prophet (*pbuh*)?

Moreover, the language itself and the circumstantial evidence support our view. First of all, in this narration الـورق بـالذهب ربا (exchange of silver with gold is *riba*), though silver and gold in equal weight cannot be exchanged, because the quantity of silver must always be higher. Secondly, the language of the *hadith* indicates that ᶜUmar did not believe in *riba al-fadl* and does not regard hand-to-hand deal as *riba* as is apparent from the words إلا هاء وهاء (except when [the exchange] is hand-to-hand) and there was no situation of credit or borrowing here. Instead, it was a hand-to-hand deal with a slight delay till the servant comes. So probability supports the view that Faruq the Great must have stated that precept of the Prophet (*pbuh*) which instructs face-to-face transaction in case of *muratalah* and *bay' sarf* and instructs ولا تبيعوا منها غائبا بناجز (and do not exchange what is present with what is not) so that every party gets the opportunity to inspect each other's commodity and evaluate it. These are the reasons why we are firm in our belief that this narration in its present wording is not the words of 'Umar. The narration in its present form is that of later narrators. Even if they are the words of 'Umar, they are not a *shar'i* rule. Rather it is an opinion based on extreme care and piety, because on another occasion 'Umar himself has said فدعوا الربا والريبة (so give up *riba* and anything that you doubt). Here in this case, there was the delay till the servant came back and it was not exactly a hand-to-hand dealing, so only for the sake of extreme caution 'Umar asked Talha to wait till the servant returned and then strike the deal, and narrated another *hadith* in support of hand-to-hand dealing only. It was not his intention to use other parts of that *hadith* related to *riba*.

So far we have quoted those *ahadith* that are used by *fuqaha* to make inferences about the prohibition of *riba*. We hope that after reading the foregoing pages, any person of a just nature cannot deny that the portions in these narrations which are the actual words of the Prophet (*pbuh*) have nothing to do with *riba* and it is certain that this is not *the riba* that was prohibited through the revelation which will be explained in the following pages. However, so far the views have been expressed as an academic discourse, otherwise the instances of *riba al-fadl* are very rare and many great 'ulama of the Ummah do not believe in *riba al-fadl*.

# 16.
# A review of the *ahadith*
## regarding *riba al-nasi'ah* (credit usury)

Now we will quote the narrations that are used as an argument against *riba al-nasi'ah* (credit usury). These narrations are of two kinds: (1) those in which *riba* has been defined or explained in a part of a sentence as a matter of a rule; (2) those narrations that describe details of incidents and contain quotes of the Prophet's (*pbuh*) instructions regarding them. Obviously, the latter form is preferable, and, therefore, such narrations have been arranged to be mentioned later.

### Hadith No. 1

عن سعيد بن المسيب : أن رسول الله صلى الله عليه وسلم قـال: لا ربا إلا في ذهب أو فضة أو مما يكال أو يوزن ويؤكل ويشرب (سنن الدارقطني، كتاب البيوع ، رقم الحديث ٢٨١٠ ، ج ٣ ، ص ١١) .

Sa'id ibn al-Musayyib narrates that the Prophet of Allah, upon whom be peace, said: There is no *riba* except in gold or silver or in such things that are sold in measures or weighed or eaten or drunk.

The style of the passage itself indicates that the narrator has mentioned his inference in a part of the sentence which is not the Prophet's (*pbuh*) words. So see the following statement about this narration.:

قال أبو الحسن هذا مرسل ووهم لمبارك على مـالك برفعه إلى النبي صلى الله عليه وسلم وإنما هو قول سعيد بن المسيب.

Abul Hasan said: this narration does not reach upto the Prophet (*pbuh*). Mubarak presumed that Malik narrated it on the strength of a chain of narrators leading upto the

Prophet (*pbuh*). In fact it is a saying by Sa'id ibn al-Musayyib.[20]

## Hadith No. 2

حدثني أسامة بن زيد أن رسول الله صلى الله عليه وسلم قال : لا
ربا إلا في النسيئة (النسائي، كتاب البيوع ، ج ٧، ص ٢٨١) .

Usamah ibn Zayd narrated that the Prophet, *pbuh*, said 'There is no *riba* except in credit dealings.'

This narration is also reported in the same words by Ibn ʿAbbas about which ʿ*Allamah* Al-Tahawi says:

تأويل حديث ابن عباس رضي الله عنهما عن أسامة رضي الله عنه
أن ذلك الربا إنما عنى به ربا القرآن ، الذي كان أصله في النسيئة ،
وذلك أن الرجل كان يكون له على صاحبه الدَّين ، فيقول له:
أجِّلني منه إلى كذا وكذا بكذا وكذا درهما أزيدكها في دَينك (أبو
جعفر الطحاوي ، **شرح معاني الآثار** ، كتاب الصرف ، باب الربا ، ط. دار
الكتب العلمية ، بيروت ، ١٩٩٦ ، ج ٤ ، ص ٦٥).

The explanation of Ibn ʿAbbas' *hadith* is that he meant the *riba* described in the Qur'an which in its origin was in credit [dealings]. It was like this: someone had a debt due on another person, the borrower asks the creditor: 'give me some more time for repayment and I will increase so many *dirhams* in your loan.'

The meaning of this *hadith* is that it refers to the *riba* prohibited by the Qur'an which is really in credit dealings, that is, someone owes a debt to someone else which becomes payable and the borrower is unable to pay. In such a circumstance the borrower requests the creditor to give

---

[20] I will submit that it is not the statement of even Sa'id ibn al-Musayyib. Instead, some later narrator has mixed up positions of the Hanafi and Shafi'i *fiqhs* and has added أو يشرب (or drunk) on his own, for literary embellishment of the text, and narrated it, because nobody believes in *riba* in drinking things like water or milk.

him leave for a particular period and promises to pay a certain amount over and above the original debt as a compensation.

This very narration by Usama has been narrated in *Sahih Muslim* in these words:

لا ربا فيما كان يدا بيـد (صحيح مسلم ، كتاب المساقاة ، رقم الحديث

۱۰۳، ج ٢ ، ص ١٢١٨).

There is no *riba* in hand-to-hand dealings.

In addition to this, there are a host of narrations that contain the wordings: لا ربا إلا في الدَّين (there is no *riba* except in credit/loan). These narrations also seem to be inferred but traditionally or rationally there is no objection to their correctness and these narrations demolish the self-invented castle of *riba al-fadl*.

One point regarding these narrations is noteworthy, that their literal translation is only this much: *riba* can occur only in credit dealings or in respect of an earlier debt. Thus the opposite of this general rule will not be a general rule; that is, in all cases of *riba* there must be credit or loan dealing but it does not mean that taking an increase in every case of credit dealing will amount to *riba*. Every donkey walks on earth but everyone that walks on earth is not a donkey. Unfortunately, this very mistake has occurred in a narration by inference. There is a narration in *Mishkat Sharif*: 'every loan earning a profit is *riba*' كل قرض جر نفعا فهـو ربا[21]. The language of this narration clearly indicates that it is not a saying of the Prophet (*pbuh*), rather it is the inference of a narrator. If borrowing means all sorts of borrowing, whatever be the purpose of borrowing and the status of the borrower, then the narrator has certainly made a mistake in understanding

---

[21] We did not find such a '*hadith*' in the chapter on *riba* in the *Mishkat al-masabih*. It seems that it is a saying of a *faqih* because *Radd al-muhtar* records the following: وفى الأشباه: كل قرض جر نفعا فهو حرام (it is said in the book *Al-Ashbah* [*wa'l-naza'ir*?] that every loan earning a profit is unlawful): Ibn ʿAbidin, *Radd al-muhtar, sharh tanwir al-absar*, Kitab al-buyuʿ, Bab al-murabahah wa'l-tawliyah, Beirut: Dar al-Kutub al-ʿilmiyah, 1994, vol. 7, pp. 294f (ed.).

83

the intent of the fore-mentioned *hadith* and he has assumed the opposite as the rule although authentic *ahadith* contradict this rule. The Prophet himself borrowed a camel with the promise to return two camels. *Sahaba* have paid more than the original amount at the time of repayment and the Prophet (*pbuh*) approved of it. If 'borrowing' means that loan which a really needy Muslim or a *dhimmi* in *Dar al-Islam* raises from a rich Muslim then, no doubt, taking a profit is prohibited. This will be discussed in detail below.

Here some of those *ahadith* must be mentioned wherein the word *riba* occurs repeatedly and which are used by some of our *fuqaha* to prove their definition of *riba* on borrowing. These narrations are generally in the form of simple statements and if minor difference are overlooked the sample of the language will be like the following:

التمر بالتمر ربا إلا هاء وهاء، والشعير بالشعير ربا إلا هاء وهاء، والحنطة بالحنطة ربا إلا هاء وهاء، والملح بالملح ربا إلا هاء وهاء، والفضة بالفضة ربا إلا هاء وهاء، والذهب بالذهب ربا إلا هاء وهاء.

Selling dates with dates is *riba* except [in] hand-to-hand [dealing]; selling barley with barley is *riba* except [in] hand-to-hand [dealing]; selling wheat with wheat is *riba* except [in] hand-to-hand [dealing]; selling salt with salt is *riba* except [in] hand-to-hand [dealing]; selling silver with silver is *riba* except [in] hand-to-hand [dealing]; and selling gold with gold is *riba* except [in] hand-to-hand [dealing].

Here, too, the style of the language indicates that these are not the words of the Prophet (*pbuh*), because had it been the Prophet's orders it would have invariably been in the form of a command or interdiction. So most probably the instructions given by the Prophet (*pbuh*) regarding exchange of dates or silver and gold ware at the time of the conquest of Khaybar or after that or the instructions given by him about the exchange of coins which have been mentioned above in some detail, have been mixed up by the narrators with the *hadith* لا ربا إلا في النسيئة (There is no *riba* except in credit dealings) and thus a new set of rules has been made up. The narrators presented their inferences as a saying of the Prophet (*pbuh*) because these narrations are generally narrated by the same people, *i.e.*, Abu Sa'id al-Khudari, Abu Hurayrah, 'Ubadah ibn al-Samit and these blessed companions are the first narrators of the above mentioned reports. Even if we suppose that these sayings are the very words of the Prophet (*pbuh*), it will have to be seen whether any *fiqhi* rule can be deduced from these *ahadith* or not.

But before presenting our own view, it would be appropriate to have a look at the opinions of earlier *fuqaha*. You have seen the inference of the Hanafis and you also know that they have not relied on these *ahadith*, otherwise they would not have believed in *riba* in hand-to-hand dealings. In fact, they base their inference on those narrations wherein narrators themselves have included their inferences as the actual narration which include words like فإذا اختلفت الأصناف فبيعوا كيف شئتم (when the commodities vary, sell as you may like).

We have shown in the foregoing pages in detail that such narrations are not reliable to make an inference. However, with the present narrations, our *fuqaha* argue for the applicability of the 'rules' of commodity-for-commodity, measure and weight.

85

## 17.
# Mistakes of the first inference

The wordings in the *ahadith* are as follows: التمر بالتمر والشـــعير بالشـــعير (dates for dates and barley for barley) which indicates that there is *riba* only in exchange of *commodity-with-commodity*. This argument is apparently very strong, so all *fuqaha,* with the exception of the Zahirites, maintain that commodity-with-commodity exchange is a condition for the occurrence of *riba*. But after a little pondering the fallacy of this argument becomes apparent for the following reasons:

1.  The opposite of a positive rule is not a negative rule, so even if it is accepted that an increase in the exchange of a commodity with commodity on credit will always be *riba,* then it is not necessary that whenever there is no commodity-for-commodity there will be no *riba* as well. So had the intention of the Prophet (*pbuh*) been what *fuqaha* have understood, the wording of the *hadith* should have been like this:

    لا ربا إلا في بيع الجنس بالجنس إذا كان نسيئة

    There is no *riba* except in selling commodity with commodity on credit.

2.  Now, as for the excess in the exchange of commodity with commodity, will it always be *riba*. It is against the *ijtihad* of the *fuqaha* themselves because in that case giving or taking two camels for one, or two houses for one, two *bighas* of land for one *bigha,* two armours for one armour, will also have to be included in *riba,* although no *faqih* considers this kind of deals as '*riba*.'

3.  Had it been the intent of the *Shariʿah* to determine every case of the excess in commodity-with-commodity dealing as '*riba*' then why should the Prophet (*pbuh*)

have enumerated only the 'six commodities'[22] for he did not say that 'commodity-for-commodity is *riba*.' Did the Prophet (*pbuh*) not know the word جنس (commodity/kind) or was this word not in use in Arabia?

4. Had the Prophet (*pbuh*) intended to prescribe a general rule about the definition of *riba* through these *ahadith* then the *sahaba*, may Allah bless them all, had greater opportunity to understand it than the *fuqaha* [who came centuries later]. Then why should Faruq the Great have said that the Prophet (*pbuh*) passed away before having explained the verse on the prohibition of *riba*?

5. Making *riba* conditional with 'commodity-for-commodity,' or considering every case of commodity-for-commodity' dealing as '*riba*,' invites many rational objections to the tenets of the *Shariʿah*.

## 18.
## Details of the second inference

On the basis of the six commodities enumerated by the Prophet (*pbuh*) there arises another question: why only these 'six commodities' were named? There were other things also that were bartered in Arabia both in kind and on credit, such as, camel, sword, armour, clothes etc. The

---

22  The 'six commodities' are: barley, wheat, dates, salt, gold and silver.

Prophet (*pbuh*) could have named those things as well. *Fuqaha* have given different answers to this question:

(a)  *ᶜAllamah* Dawud al-Zahiri and other *Zahirites*[23] opine that there is *riba* only in these six things, *i.e.*, barley wheat dates, salt, gold and silver, and there is no *riba* in the remaining things.

The only rational objection to this opinion is that rice, pulses, sugar have the same qualities that are found in barley and wheat etc., then why is there no *riba* in them? This is the reason why other *fuqaha* have looked for other reasons.

(b)  According to *Imam* Shafiᶜi, may Allah bless him, edibility is the cause of *riba* in the first four of the mentioned articles, and valuability [bearing a value] is the reason in the remaining two.

There are two objections to this definition: there are many other things which have edibility such as meat, vegetables, fruits, milk. Then why did the Holy Prophet not mention them?

Secondly, no *common* reason for these six things has been mentioned. Otherwise every thing has one or the other distinctive quality.

(c)  In order to eliminate these objections, Hanafi *fuqaha* traced a common feature in the 'six commodities,' that is, measurability and weighbility, and held this to be the reason for *riba*.

But the fallacy of this approach is so obvious that it does not require much argument. We admit that those six commodities were sold by weight or by measures, but this common feature should have something common with *riba*. The *logic* here is this: all crows are forbidden and all crows are black, so the black colour is the reason for prohibition!

However, in the foregoing pages we have written enough about the wrong results of holding

---

23  The *Zawahir* الظواهر, or *ahl al-zahair* أهل الظاهر, are the followers of the Zahiri school of Islamic *fiqh* which does not believe in inference (*qiyas*) and sticks to the apparent and obvious (*zahir* ظاهر) meanings of the Islamic legal texts. The leader of this school was Dawud ibn Khalaf al-Zahiri (d. 270H/883-4CE) (ed.).

measurability and weighability as the condition for *riba* and this need not be repeated here.

(d) In the opinion of *Imam* Malik, may Allah bless him, there is *riba* in storable [non-perishable] edibles only and there is no *riba* in any other commodity. As for gold and silver mentioned in the *hadith*, it is secondary, that is, in itself it is not a cause for *riba* but as they are used as a means to buy storable [non-perishable] edibles so they have been mentioned in the *hadith* as a means to buy non-perishable edibles.

# 19.
## Reasons for *riba* in storable edibles

No doubt this opinion is closest to the correct position. But the *Imam* [Malik], may Allah bless him, has not given any reason why the *Shariah* considers *riba* in storable [non-perishable] edibles and why not in other things. The details, in our opinion, are as follows:

The intent of the *Shariah* is that wherever there is an Islamic state the poor and the needy should not go without food and those who are not wealthy but have self-respect and do not like to accept charities (*sadaqah* and *Zakat*) and in order to feed their family, purchase cereals on credit or borrow money from the rich to buy food, these people should get a grace period till they are financially well off and the creditor should not be given an opportunity to exploit such needy persons.

Since 'need' has a broad meaning which is likely to occur to a king as well as a beggar. So in the *Shariah* 'need' means that need without which the very survival of life may not be possible, that is, food which is a must for survival. This is the reason why only those things are mentioned in these *ahadith* that were used as food among the ancient Arabs. Those things were not counted as food which could not be stored in those days such as meat, fish, or such fruits that could not be dried and preserved, because no one would retain such things with an intention to sell them after their season ends and thus make an undue profit by selling them to the needy. For example, in our country there are plenty of mangoes, some people consider it against their prestige to sell them and as Indians so far do not know any technique to preserve them, they are compelled to distribute them among their friends. On the contrary, if there is an excess production of cereals, people preserve them so that in winter, when the poor have used up their cereals and rates have gone up, they would earn higher profits due to the demand of the needy or as a result of the increased rates. Islam has forbidden withholding such basic necessities of life. The warnings against *ihtikar* (hoarding)[24] and denial of

---

[24] Buying up of things, which are generally used as edibles, at a time when they are cheap and collecting them from everywhere and selling them when they become dearer is called *Ihtikar* احتكار in the terminology of the *Shariʿah*. Hoarding is unlawful under the *Shariʿah*. See the following narrations for instance:

*(a)*:

(ا) عن سعيد بن المسيب عن عمر قال رسول الله صلى الله عليه وسلم : 'المحتكر ملعون' (**ابن ماجة** ، كتاب التجارات ، باب الحكرة والجلب ، رقم الحديث ٢١٥٣، ج ٢ ، ص ٧٢٨).

Saʿid ibn al-Musayyib narrates through ʿUmar that the Prophet (*pbuh*) said that the one who held back cereals so that it became dearer is cursed.

*(b)*:

(ب) عن أبي أمامة نهى رسول الله صلى الله عليه وسلم أن يُحتكر الطعام.
[عن أبي أمامة أن رسول الله صلى الله عليه وسلم قال : من احتكر طعاما أربعين يوما ثم تصدق به لم تكن له كفارة . رواه رزين : **مشكاة المصابيح** ، كتاب البيوع ، باب الاحتكار ، ج ١ ، ص ٢٥١].

Abu Umamah says that the Prophet (*pbuh*) forbade the hoarding of food to make it dearer.
[It is narrated on the authority of Abu Umamah that the Prophet, upon whom be peace, said: Whoever hoarded food for forty days and then gave it in charity, this will not suffice him as atonement].

*ma'un* ماعون (implements/utensils)[25] and the instructions in *ahadith* about waiving the debts of the indigent and the

---

*(c)*:

(ج)  عن أبي هريرة قال رسول اللـه صلى اللـه عليه وسلم : "من احتكر، يريد أن
يتغالى بها على المسلمين، فهو خاطئ وقد برئ منه ذمة اللـه"
[عن معمر قال: قال رسول الله صلى الله عليه وسلم : من احتكر فهو خاطئ:
صحيح مسلم ، كتاب المساقاة ، باب تحريم الاحتكار في الأقوات، رقم الحديث
١٦٠٥ ، ج ٢، ص ١٢٢٧].

Abu Hurayrah narrated that the Prophet (*pbuh*) said: Whoever underline{withholds} [food] underline{in order to make it dearer for Muslims} is a sinner and God is not responsible for him. [Mu'ammar narrated that the Prophet of Allah, peace be upon him, said: Whoever hoards is a sinner].

In the last quoted *hadith* the underlined words indicate that the instruction wherein charity has been made obligatory is exclusively for needy Muslims or those equal to them such as *dhimmis*.

*(d)*:

(د)  قال أبو داؤد : سألت أحمد ما الحكرة ؟، قال : "ما فيه عيش الناس" (أبو داؤد،
كتاب البيوع ، باب فى النهي عن الحكرة ، رقم الحديث ٣٤٤٧ ، ج ٣، ص
٢٧١).

Abu Dawud said: I asked Ahmad what is hoarding? He replied: it is [withholding] things which are means of human survival.

*(e)*:

(هـ)  قال الأوزاعي : "المحتكر من يعترض السوق" (أبو داؤد ، كتاب البيوع ،
باب فى النهي عن الحكرة ، رقم الحديث ٣٤٤٧ ، ج ٣ ، ص ٢٧١).

*Imam* Awza'i said: The hoarder is the one who plays up with the market.

---

[25]  Literally, *ma'un* ماعون means things of necessity/utility. In the terminology of *Shari'ah* two types of things are called *ma'un*. One, natural products at their natural sources, such as water in the river or stream, wood in the forest, salt in its mine, etc. According to Islamic law these things in nature are nobody's property and everybody has the right to use them. The ruler or the landlord has no right to set conditions for using them. It is narrated in an authentic (*sahih*) *hadith* that a person asked the Prophet (*pbuh*):

يا رسول الله ! ما الشئ الذي لا يحل منعه، قال : الماء . قال : يا نبي الله ! ما الشئ
الذي لا يحل منعه، قال : الملح" (أبو داؤد ، كتاب الزكاة ، باب ما لا يجوز منعه ،
رقم الحديث ١٦٦٩ ، ج ٢ ، ص ١٢٧).

O Prophet of God! what is the thing the withholding of which is unlawful. He replied: Water. Again he asked: what

91

bankrupt for which *muhaddithun* have a separate chapter under the title باب من أفلس (chapter on the bankrupt) are, in fact, a piece of this chain.

However, the *hadith* presently under consideration seems to indicate that in the dealings of these commodities the increase on the actual debt is *riba* in every case. It may be submitted in this respect that even if these narrations are taken as the sayings of the Prophet (*pbuh*), the purpose of the narration is not to provide a general logical rule. Rather, they are concerned with the credit dealings prevalent in those days among the Arabs. In fact, everywhere in the early stages of civilisation, when people take edible commodities on credit, the creditor himself would dictate the terms of the agreement for the return of the commodity later with an increase. In Indian villages even today cereals

---

is the thing the withholding of which is not lawful? He said: Salt.

Now there are man-made things which are needed at times but it is not possible for the poor to keep them or acquire them, such as big cauldrons, carpets or palanquins which are needed in ceremonies. Borrowing of these things is *ma'un*. Whoever has it is bound to lend it to the needy.

Similarly, there are instructions about the indebted poor, that is, he should go to the *Qadi* and declare his debts and place his assets in the custody of the *Qadi*, who will call the creditors and distribute the assets among them according to their share, and the remaining debt will be forgiven so that the person in debt becomes free to re-start his business. The current law of bankruptcy is based on this very principle of the *Shari'ah*.

This argument clarifies the fact that the reason for the proscription of *riba* in the case of dates, wheat, barley and salt, is not the quality of these things itself, that is, their being edibles, but the real reason is the fact that the poor and the incapable people are compelled to borrow these things for their survival, or in the case of *bay' salaf* they are unable to repay on time according to the agreement. So among the storable [non-perishable] ماكولات مُدَّخرة edibles only those things are mentioned that are staple food. Edibles consumed by the rich, such as olive oil, or honey or walnut and almonds are edibles and storable but even their names do not appear in the *ahadith* although these things were used as food in Arabia.

92

are lent to be returned with an increase of a quarter or a half. Here barley, peas and wheat are normal edible commodities, while in Arabia dates were used as staple food. Salt, an essential ingredient of food, was scarce in Arabia.

## 20.
## Prevalent practices of interest

Now we have to see what was the prevalent practice of dealings on credit in Arabia and whether the present interest-based dealings were found in Arabia or not. The examples we have unearthed after research and enquiries show that the present practices of interest-based business were not known in Arabia.

Today the following methods of interest are prevailing. The first method is that someone borrows money from another person on the condition that the lending person will get a certain percentage of the amount monthly or annually in addition to the actual amount as a charge for the use of his money by the borrower. Borrowing is either for commercial and industrial purposes or for the personal use of the borrower. If it is for the former purpose the excess amount is called 'interest' and if it is for the latter it is called 'usury.'[26]

---

[26] The excess amount paid on money borrowed for commercial purposes is called 'interest' in English. And if it is borrowed for personal use, which generally bears a higher rate of interest, this excess is called 'usury.'

Another practice of the interest-based dealings is that a trader borrows on credit some commercial commodities from another trader, or a customer buys something for personal use from a shopkeeper and promises to pay the price after a certain period. In that case the seller increases a certain percentage in the price of the commodities in accordance with the length of the agreed grace period and tells the customer, for instance, that the price is *rupees* one hundred if you pay it today and if you pay after a month the price will be *rupees* one hundred and five, if you pay in two months it will be one hundred and ten, and so on and so forth.

A third form of interest-based business is that some persons or a company or government organisation keeps other peoples' savings with them safely and helps traders by making payments to them at various places, as well as lending that money to others. Thus providing finances is their business, on the one hand, and, on the other hand, they pay a substantial fixed amount out of their income to those who deposit their money with them. This sort of business practice is called 'banking.' This practice was not prevalent in Arabia.

## 21.
### *Riba* practices in early Arabia: *bay<sup>c</sup> salaf* and *riba*

The prevalent practice in those days in Arabia was more or less like what we have nowadays in our villages where grain is lent against an excess of a quarter or a half. The only difference is that if some one lends a *maund* of grain, at the same time he extracts from the borrower a promise to return one and a half or two *maunds* at the time of the next harvest.

But in Arabia they did not enter into any agreement of this sort at the time of borrowing. Instead, it used to be a kind of an advance purchase. For example, today we pay some money as an advance price and purchase grain not yet cropped or lend some grain and agree to get back the same quantity of grain or the total produce of the next harvest of a particular field. If the grain thus purchased earlier is received on time as promised and the debt is cleared, the creditor will be satisfied with that. But if the borrower could not keep his promise on time, then the lender or the advance purchaser will have the right to increase the price or the quantity by a half or even double, as a charge for the extra time allowed by him. The Arabs called the original deal as *bay' salaf,* and this increase which was not agreed at the beginning of the deal and, only later, in the case of unkept promise, depended solely on the discretion of the creditor. This second form was called *riba* about which we have quoted *'Allamah* Al-Tahawi's opinion[27] which includes: لا ربا إلا فى النسيئة (there is no *riba* except in credit dealings). The last part of *'Allamah* Al-Tahawi's quotation says: فيكون مشتريا للأجل بمال (so he buys a grace period by paying money), *i.e.*, the money received as a compensation for the extension of the loan period is *riba*. In other words, *riba* is a compensation for the deferment of a due payment which depends on the discretion of the creditor in the case of the non-fulfilment of the promise.

Now, there can be a doubt that this is what 'interest' is all about, because 'interest' is an amount which the borrower has to pay to the creditor according to the amount of borrowed money and the length of the borrowing period. Then what is the difference between the two? True, apparently there is no difference. But in reality there is a big difference.

According to the practice prevailing in Arabia there used to be no agreement for an increase at the time of the deal. The borrower made the deal in the hope that he would be

---
[27] See page 82 above.

able to repay the due at the appointed time and when he failed to repay on time for whatever reason the creditor would double the amount in lieu of the time allowed and the borrower had to agree. Had it been stated at the very beginning that in case the money or capital was not returned within such and such period till that time such and such payment would have to be made monthly or annually, it was quite likely that the borrower would not make the deal on that condition. But after concluding the deal and the borrower being unable to fulfil the promise, there was no scope for undoing the deal. In such a case the agreement for the increase would be completely one-sided which is blatant exploitation.

After further investigation, it becomes clear that such a deal, *bayᶜ salaf*, was generally contracted by the indigent and the poor. They, for the sake of their survival, used to take food items, such as barley, wheat or dates before the crop would be ready or would borrow *dirhams* and *dinars* in order to buy those things and thus sold in advance their next crop. When the next crop became ready, the buyer, who was in fact the creditor, would come to take possession of the ready crop. If the borrower would give away the crop according to the earlier promise, he would not have been left with any thing for sustenance, so he would give part of the produce and the buyer would allow him a further period for returning the remaining balance on condition that its quantity would be increased. This is what *Imam* Al-Baghawi has said in his *tafsir, Maᶜalim al-tanzil*, while interpreting the *ayah* on the proscription of *riba*.

## 22.
# *Imam* al-Baghawi's interpretation of the *riba* verse

قال عطاء وعكرمة : نزلت في العبـاس بـن عبدالمطلب وعثمـان بـن
عفان رضي الله عنهما، وكانا قد أسلفا في التمر، فلما حضر الجـذاذ
قال لهما صـاحب التمـر : إن أنتمـا أخذتمـا حقكمـا لا يبقـي لي مـا
يكفي عيالي، فهل لكما أن تأخذا النصف وتؤخرا النصف وأضعِف
لكما، ففعلا . فلما حل الأجل طلبا الزيادة، فبلغ ذلك رسـول الله
صلى الله عليه وسلم فنهاهما، فأنزل الله تعالى هذه الآية (معالم التنزيل
(مطبوع مع تفسير الخازن)، ج ١، ص ٣٨٩) .

ᶜAta and ᶜIkrama say that this verse was revealed in
connection with [the dealings] of Al-ᶜAbbas ibn ᶜAbd
al-Muttalib and ᶜUthman, may Allah be pleased with
them. These persons used to make advance deals about
dates before the ripening of the crop [*i.e.,* they used to buy
dates in advance with cash or with dates]. After the
ripening of dates the owner would say that if you took
away your right, nothing would be left for the sustenance
of my family; would you agree to take only half of the
agreed quantity and leave the remaining half which I will
pay in double quantity next season. So they agreed to this.
When the appointed time came, they demanded the
increase. When the Prophet (*pbuh*) heard about it he
prohibited it and the said verse was revealed.

This is why a great scholar opines that there is *riba* in *bayᶜ
salaf* only.

Now we have reached a point where we can define *the riba*
in the Qur'anic perspective and that of the
occasion/circumstances of its revelation and in the light of
authentic *ahadith*. It is also possible now to say which
conditions among those put forward by various *fuqaha* for
*riba* are correct and to what extent, and if there has been
any mistake, what are the causes for it, and also under the
present circumstances which method could be in
accordance with the Holy Qur'an and the Prophet's (*pbuh*)

97

tradition. With this objective in view certain important points, which have been mentioned earlier as a foreword and may have slipped from memory, are briefly restated here.

## 23.
## Irrationality of the definition of *riba* by *fuqaha*

The definition of *riba* by some *fuqaha* is clearly against rationality and justice for the following reasons:

1. The condition of exchanging commodity-with-commodity does away with the very purpose which was the basic cause of forbidding *riba*, that is, the rich should be compelled to meet the needs of the poor, and taking any compensation for that moral benevolence be declared unlawful.

2. In case of commodity-for-commodity exchange, failure to keep the difference between genuine and spurious, between good and bad, is clearly against reason and justice.

3. Linking *riba* with measure and weight invites the above-mentioned first objection. Moreover, rules of the permanent *Shari'ah* become subject to our changing traditions.

4. In case of the exchange of manufactured or high quality commodities, disregard of the workmanship charges or value added to the quality is also clearly against rationality.

5. In hand-to-hand deals an increase is impossible and if there is an increase it will be due to the difference in the value of the two commodities, so this definition of *riba*,

which applies to this kind of deals, will also certainly be wrong.

6. Suppose this definition of *riba* is accepted as correct, a slight change of wordings will render all present day interest-based dealings 'lawful' and permissible and out of the purview of the definition of *riba*. In such circumstances, how far it will be justified to describe 'interest' as synonymous with '*riba*?'

## 24.
## Rules must vary in accordance with differences in deals, persons and situations

Reason and justice demand that the rules should vary according to the variation in the purpose of the deal, persons involved in the deal and the geographical location of the deal. These factors have not been taken into consideration in this definition. Details of this objection are as follows:

### (a) Purpose of the deal

Suppose a person takes a loan for commercial business or to purchase a land-holding or to travel to Europe; and the purpose of his loan is to earn profit, seek prestige or to enjoy a luxury. Another person has many dependants, is sick, has nothing to eat and takes a loan for his treatment and survival and for caring for his minor children. The rules should vary in these two conditions.

## (b) Parties to the deal

Suppose there is a Muslim or a *dhimmi* person: if he is a creditor he cannot take *riba* from us and doing benevolence to him is a religious duty of ours. There is another person, a non-Muslim: if he lends us money he would certainly charge, or could charge, us *riba*, and with whom we have no agreement not to give or take *riba* from one another; neither is it our duty to do benevolence to him. Rather doing benevolence to him in certain circumstances would be suicidal to the *Ummah* and would deprive our Islamic brethren of their right. Non-differentiation between these two circumstances can never be the intent of the *Shariʿah*.

## (c) Location of the deal

*Dar al-Islam* is the place where Islamic rules are enforced and where we cannot be forced to pay *riba*. *Dar al-kufr* is the place where we do not have our government and where by law we may be bound to pay *riba*, where we may be allowed to perform our religious obligations or where a few rules of our religion could be implemented on certain conditions, while in all other remaining matters the rules of the non-believers would be openly enforced, and as Muslims, our status may be, at best, that of a resident with permission from the authorities. For a rule, which relates to the mutual behaviour of people, to be equally applicable at both places disregarding the different conditions, is against reason.

## 25.
## Details of objections to 'b' and 'c'

Items 'b' and 'c' of the above objections do not apply to Hanafi *fuqaha*, may Allah bless them. Following are the reasons for it being wrong:

1. Certain narrations regarding *muratalah* (barter) or *bay^c sarf* (exchange of coins) stated by the Prophet (*pbuh*) at the time of the conquest of Khaybar in accordance with the requirements of the circumstances, were taken as *legal* rules and were applied to *riba* for no reason, such as the matter of the Khaybar dates or the matter of the sale of gold and silver booty on the day of the conquest of Khaybar.

2. Some narrations of later narrators about the above mentioned events are inferred and not actual sayings of the Prophet. Some of the narrators have mixed up narrations regarding *muratalah* and *bay^c sarf* and have presented their personal opinions or the inferences of earlier narrators as the sayings of the Prophet (*pbuh*).

3. After the demise of the Prophet (*pbuh*), a certain *sahabi* made an objection to a particular case and mentioned a *hadith* to validate his stand. While only a portion of that *hadith* was intended to support the *sahabi*'s stand at the time, *fuqaha* applied the *whole hadith* to the matter at hand. For example, the matter of the *hadith* quoted by ^cUmar al-Faruq.

4. A certain *sahabi* raised an objection in a particular matter because due to his wrong inference he believed it to be improper. But although the words he quoted as those of the Prophet (*pbuh*) were correct, his inference was wrong. In later inferred narrations the saying of the *sahabi* and the wordings of the Prophet (*pbuh*) got mixed up and were narrated later as the sayings of the Prophet (*pbuh*) himself. Later even personal opinions of narrators down the line were also included in it to become a part of the whole, such as the matter of ^cUbadah ibn al-Samit's *khutbah*.

## 26.
## Sayings of *sahaba* and inferences of *fuqaha* are mixed up with *ahadith* of the Prophet

Following are our arguments for the above-mentioned inferences:

*(a)* The narrations are made with reference to a particular *sahabi*. But the narrations by the same *sahabi* about the same event are found in different ways in authentic books of *Hadith*. The texts of various narrations differ from each other and sometimes are contradictory. Now the common values in all such narrations can be believed to be true but the words that occur in one narration and do not occur in another narration may not necessarily be correct.

*(b)* Even in the common value the style of the language indicates how much of it is the saying of the Prophet (*pbuh*) and how much the opinion of a *sahabi* himself.

*(c)* The superfluous and unrelated piece(s) of the text is/are even otherwise wrong because the Prophet (*pbuh*) gave instructions about *muratalah* and *bay$^c$ sarf* during the days of Khaybar while till that time *riba* had not been proscribed.

*(d)* If those instructions were legislative, then the Holy Qur'an, while proscribing *riba* on credits/loans, would also have proscribed these forms of '*riba*.' As the verse proscribing *riba* was revealed *after* the narrations about the occurrence of *riba* in the case of excess in hand-to-hand deals, those *ahadith* must be treated as invalidated by Qur'anic verses. The assertion of some revered persons, that *ahad*[28] *ahadith* explain Qur'anic injunctions, is simply wrong, for how could the

---

28 *Hadith ahad* [*aahaad*] حديث آحاد (single *hadiths*) means narration(s) by one or a few companions of the Prophet (*pbuh*) as against '*mutawatir* متواتر *hadiths* which are narrated by a large number of the companions and, therefore, are considered definite proofs of a certain rule of Islamic law, while the former [*hadith ahad*] are not (ed.).

Prophet's sayings interpret or explain yet-to-be-revealed verses of the Qur'an?

*(e)* If these narrations are held as correct, the excess in hand-to-hand deals will also be *riba*, whereas narrations by highly respected *sahaba* like ʿUmar al-Faruq, Zayd ibn al-Arqam, Usama ibn Zayd, ʿAbdallah ibn ʿAbbas, may Allah be pleased with them, contradict this.

*(f)* The narrations by these venerable companions of the Prophet (*pbuh*) prove that *riba* occurs in the deals on credit or loans only.

*(g)* The *'riba'* prevalent in Arabia was in *bayʿ salaf* transactions and, at the time of the deal, there used to be no condition/promise for an eventual increase. When the buyer on credit or the debtor, due to his inability, failed to repay at the appointed time, he agreed, under the sheer pressure of the creditor, to an increase over the original amount. This excess amount was called *'riba'* by Arabs. This is apparent from the circumstances of the revelation of the verses proscribing *riba*.

*(h)* If it is supposed that these *ahadith* are related to *riba* and that one kind of it is *riba al-fadl* [*riba* in hand-to-hand dealing] which, according to *fuqaha*, is forbidden by the Prophet (*pbuh*), even then it will be out of the purview of our discussion, for later *fuqaha* agree that these *hadiths* are about *riba al-fadl* and in our present-day society such cases do not occur. Thus the question does not arise today about their being permissible or non-permissible. These were submissions as a sort of academic debate.

# 27

## Narrations regarding *riba*

It is clear from the forgoing discussion that there is no *shar'i* argument to support the definition of *riba* on credit, as propounded by some *'ulama*. Rather *shar'i* texts oppose this point of view. Wordings of some narrations held by *fuqaha* as arguments in favour of the proscription of *riba* are unrelated to *'riba.'* Instead they are results of misunderstanding by later narrators. Subject to their authenticity being proven, they may be taken at the most as relating to *riba al-fadl* which is not questioned here.

There is no explanation in *Hadith* for the Qur'anic verse regarding *riba* on credit transactions for, according to 'Umar al-Faruq, the Prophet (*pbuh*) passed away without explaining this verse. So let us ourselves define *riba* after a thorough study of the Qur'anic verses and the Prophet's (*pbuh*) sayings in this respect. But before doing so, let us make a thorough study of some other authentic *ahadith*.

28.
## No *riba* between a *harbi* and a Muslim

Now there remains only one *hadith* which clearly contains the word *'riba.'* It is narrated by Mak-hul al-Shami مكحول الشامي[29]:

---

29   Al-Marghinani has mentioned this *hadith* in *al-Hidayah* (vol. 2, p. 70) where he has said that *Imam* Shafi'i and through him [Shafi'i] al-Bayhaqi has also narrated it and that *Imam* Abu Hanifah has narrated it on the authority of some of his *shaykhs* (ed.).

لا ربا بين المسلم والحربي في دار الحرب

There is no *riba* between a Muslim and a *harbi*[30] in *Dar al-harb*.

Some *fuqaha* of *Ahl al-Sunnah* do not believe this *hadith* to be authentic on the basis of the principles of narration.[31] But Hanafis take it to be authentic. However, it will be submitted later that rationally or traditionally [*i.e.*, in the light of Islamic traditions and beliefs] there is no scope for doubt in the authenticity of this *hadith* and it is supported by the Holy Qur'an itself. In this connection *Dar al-harb* will also be thoroughly discussed.

For the present only two more *ahadith* may be briefly mentioned. The word '*riba*' does not occur in them but still they throw light on the issue of *riba*.

One *hadith* is narrated by ʿAbdallah ibn ʿUmar that he borrowed one or some *dirhams* from someone. When he repaid, he gave *dirhams* of better quality and of higher value than the original loan. The creditor, himself being a *sahabi* and a God-fearing person, objected to this for fear that it could be *riba*. ʿAbdallah ibn ʿUmar replied that there was no harm in it for the Prophet (*pbuh*) himself has said:

أحسنكم أحسنكم قضاءً

The best of you is the one who is the best in repaying debts.

Another *hadith* is mentioned in *Imam* Malik's *Muwatta'* as follows:

عن مجاهد أنه قال : استسلف عبدالله بن عمر من رجل دراهم ، ثـم قضاه دراهمَ خيرا منها ، فقال الرجل: يا أبا عبدالرحمن ! هـذه خير

---

30   '*Harbi*' حربي is a resident of *dar al-harb*, that is a citizen of a non-Muslim country: see my paper '*Dar al-harb* and *Dar al-Islam*,' *Muslim & Arab Perspectives*, New Delhi, 2:11-12 (1995), pp. 51-65 (ed.).

31   This *hadith* is classified as *mursal* مرسل ('hanging') because its narrator, Mak-hul, has reported on the authority of someone he did not meet *personally* (ed.).

من دراهمي التي أسلفتك ، فقال عبدالله بن عمر : قد علمتُ ولكن
نفسي بذلك طيبة (مؤطأ الإمام مـالك ، كتـاب البيوع ، باب مـا يجـوز مـن
السلف ، رقم الحديث ١٣٧٣ ، ط. ٢ ، بيروت: دارالنفائس، ص ٤٧٤).

Mujahid narrates that ʿAbdallah ibn ʿUmar took a loan of
a few *dirhams* from someone. While repaying the loan, he
gave better *dirhams* than he had taken. The person said:
'Father of ʿAbdur Rahman! These are better than the
*dirhams* I lent you.' ʿAbdallah ibn ʿUmar said, 'yes, I
know, but I feel happy about it.'

The expression 'I feel happy about it' may be used as an
argument to claim that it was a deal with the debtor's free
will. I would submit that one and a quarter *tola* of silver
against one *rupee* is also a deal of free will: why is it held as
non-permissible? Moreover, this *hadith* supports my
argument that that deal is unlawful where the borrower,
having failed to repay the debt, had to agree under duress to
pay *riba*. Otherwise at the time of making a deal everybody
readily agrees to pay interest with the exception of a person
who is starving for want of food. This view is further
supported by the very deed of the Prophet (*pbuh*) as is
apparent from the following narration:

عن أبي هريرة رضي الله عنه قال : استقرض رسـول الله صلى الله
عليه وسلم سنّا [بعيرا] فأعطى سنا فوقه، وقال : خياركم محاسنكم
قضاءا (صحيح مسلم ، كتاب المساقاة ، باب من استسلف شيئا فقضى خيرا
منه ، رقم الحديث ١٢١ ، ج ٢ ، ص ١٢٢٥) [وفى صحيح الـترمذي، كنتاب
البيوع ، باب استقراض البعير والحيوان، ج ٦ ص ٥٦ ما يلي : عن أبي هريرة
قال : استقرض رسول الله صلى الله عليه وسلم سنّا فأعطاه سنا خيرا من سنهِ،
فقال: خياركم أحاسنكم قضاءا].

It is narrated by Abu Hurayrah that the Prophet (*pbuh*)
borrowed a two-year-old camel and returned a similar
camel, and in addition he gave another camel, and said:
'Best of you are the best in returning your debts.'

106

## 29.
# The difference between the Prophet's (pbuh) increase and the bay^c salaf of al-^cAbbas

Another narration is as follows in *Abu Dawud:*

كان لي على النبي – صلى الله عليه وسلم – دَين فقضاني وزادني

(أبو داؤد، كتاب البيوع، ج ٣، ص ٢٤٨) .

The Prophet had taken a loan from me. He repaid the loan to me and paid me an extra amount.

According to this *hadith*, it is proved by the Prophet's (*pbuh*) own words and deeds that at the time of repayment it is commendable to give over and above the original amount of loan. But as mentioned in *Tafsir Ma^calim al-Tanzil*, according to the narration of ^cIkramah, al-^cAbbas' dealing of *bay^c salaf* is unlawful and the increase is considered '*riba*,' and this very dealing has been held as the cause of the revelation of the verse proscribing *riba*. So we have to find why the deal by the Prophet (*pbuh*) is not considered *riba* and why the dealing of al-^cAbbas in the matter of advance purchase of dates was proscribed as *riba*. Following factors are common to both cases:
1. There was no agreement about an increase at the time of making the deal;
2. At the time of repayment there was an increase over the original due in both the cases;
3. In both cases there was repayment of the amount due, that is, both were cases of deals on credit.

And following factors are not common to the above-mentioned two cases:
1. One is the case of a loan and the other is a case of advance purchase. But this difference is not so fundamental as to call for different rules for each case, because whether we sell something after taking the price in advance or take a loan and promise to repay it, in both cases there is a repayable due.

107

2. A camel is involved in one case and dates in the other. If we agree to the Zahirites view that there is *riba* only in the 'six commodities,' there can be the difference of commodities. Even then the question remains: what is the rational or moral basis for specifying 'six commodities' for *riba*?

Similarly, Hanafis say that the camel are not sold by measure' or 'weight' so there is no *riba* in it. This argument is more astonishing because it has been shown earlier that there is no rational cause or *shar^c i* proof to link *riba* with 'measure' or 'weight.'

Perhaps the Shafi^c is will fail to mention any difference between the two cases, because there is edibility in the camel just as it is in wheat. One is slaughtered to make *kebabs* and the other is ground to make bread.

Now there are the Malikis. Surely, they can say that the camel as an edible cannot be stored. But still they will be asked: why is there *riba* in the storable [durable] edibles? The storability of edibles is not such a defect that could cause in its eaters immorality or physical diseases, like intoxication by liquor or brutality by eating the meat of predatory animals or diseases caused by consuming poisonous things. Then why charging an excess on loans of storable edibles is forbidden?

The only answer is that edibility and storability in themselves are not the causes for *riba*. But, because of edibility the needy is compelled to borrow them for his very survival and by storing and withholding them the rich have the opportunity to exploit the poor. So the reason, in fact, for *riba* is the need of the borrower who must survive by means of food.

The other reason is the mentality of the creditor who exploits the basic needs of the poor through storage.
3. The third difference, which could probably be used as an argument, is that in the case of the camel there was no pre-condition for the increase and in the case of the dates, although there was no agreement for *riba* in the beginning but later, when the indebted or the seller in

108

advance of his harvest would fail to fulfil his commitment on time, he was compelled to conclude an agreement for an increase on the original amount due.

In this respect it may be said first of all that none of the *fuqaha* have held that the pre-determined or the agreed increase is not necessary for it being *riba*. Secondly, what is the difference between having or not having a previously agreed deal for the increase? You may say that in the case of pre-condition there is compulsion but in the absence of the agreement it is a matter of one's free will. The answer to this is that when and if an act itself is permissible what is the harm in making an agreement about it? There is the following narration in *Abu Dawud*:

عن عبدالله بن عمرو أن رسول الله صلى الله عليه وسلم أمره أن يُجَهِّز جيشا، فنفدت الإبل، فـأمره أن يـأخذ في قلائص الصدقة . فكـان يـأخذ البعير بالبعيرين إلى إبل الصدقة (أبو داؤد، كتاب البيوع، رقم الحديث ٣٣٥٧، ج ٣، ص ٢٥٠) .

It is narrated by ͨAbdallah ibn ͨAmr that the Prophet (*pbuh*) ordered him to provide the provisions for an army. But camels were scarce so the Prophet (*pbuh*) ordered him to buy camels on credit against camels [that would come to] the treasury. So he used to take one camel against [the promise to pay] two from the camels of the treasury.

Thus the presence of a condition or its absence in itself is not the reason for proscription. However, the condition itself must be without any compulsion and with the approval of the borrower. You may ask: what would be the measure of his approval and free will? The answer is: the criterion in every just law in the world will be the criterion here also. If the person consenting to an increase is incapable, poor and helpless, that is, he is forced to borrow in order to save his life, or he is unable to repay an earlier debt on time and the creditor is not prepared to allow him any more time and, in such a situation of helplessness, he enters into an agreement, then this would be an 'agreement of the desperate' which will not be binding under Islamic

109

law as has been mentioned in the following narration in
*Abu Dawud*:

خطبنا علي بن أبي طالب أو قال : قال علي، قال عيسى : هكذا
حدثنا هُشيم قال : سيأتي على الناس زمان عضوض يعض المُوسر
على ما في يديه ولم يؤمر بذلك – قال الله تعالى : "وَلَا تَنسَوُا
الْفَضْلَ بَيْنَكُمْ" (البقرة: ٢٣٧) – ويبايع المضطرون وقد نهي النبي صلى
الله عليه وسلم عن بيع المضطر (أبو داؤد، كتاب البيوع ، رقم الحديث
٣٣٨٢ ، ح ٣، ص ٢٥٥) .

ᶜAli ibn Abi Talib gave us a sermon in which he said:
Fierce time is approaching when the rich will clinch their
fists although they have not been ordained to do so. Allah
says: 'do not forget generosity among yourselves' [2:237].
They will make deals with the desperate although the
Prophet (*pbuh*) has forbidden dealing with the desperate.

This *khutbah* of ᶜAli, may Allah honour his face, clarifies
many facts. For instance, the rich are duty-bound to help
the poor. Allah's order for mutual generosity, as the Qur'an
says 'do not forget generosity among yourselves,' shows
that the condition of mutual generosity is confined to
dealings between Muslims only. It is evident that giving up
claim to *riba*, on account of generosity and benefaction, is
unnecessary in dealings between Muslims and *harbis*.

This was the case in the story of the dates and on this
basis the agreement for the increase will be regarded by
compulsion and so it is unlawful. In the case of camels the
reason for borrowing was not to ensure survival of life and
the Prophet (*pbuh*) was not compelled to borrow at these
terms. If the creditor wanted an agreement for an increase
and the Prophet (*pbuh*) did not like it, he could have refused
it. But if he accepted with pleasure that condition would
not be unlawful, for just as the repayment of a loan with an
increase is a laudable principle, similarly making a promise
to do this commendable act would not amount to a sin.

The following conclusions are drawn from this detailed
discussion:

## 30.
# Conditions where increase is permissible and where it is not

If a loan is given to a needy person for the maintenance of his children, charging an increase or making a condition for an increase is not permissible. Or if someone is in debt and he is unable to pay it within the specified time, that is, he does not possess enough money to repay the debt or in the case of paying the debt he will not be left with enough money to provide for his children, then an agreement for an increase will not be binding because this agreement will not be considered as one made with the debtor's free will, and every increase on the actual amount in such a case will be *riba*. On the contrary, if a loan is taken for any other purpose and an agreement for an increase is made with pleasure and without any compulsion, it is not only permissible but it is laudable. A careful study of the Qur'anic verses leads us to this very conclusion. These are the verses in the Holy Qur'an about *riba*.

### (a) Zakat and *riba* compared

أَوَ لَمْ يَرَوْا أَنَّ اللهَ يَبْسُطُ الرِّزْقَ لِمَنْ يَشَاءُ وَيَقْدِرُ، إِنَّ فِيْ ذَلِكَ لَآيَاتٍ لِّقَوْمٍ يُؤْمِنُوْنَ . فَآتِ ذَا الْقُرْبَى حَقَّهُ وَالْمِسْكِيْنَ وَابْنَ السَّبِيْلِ، ذَلِكَ خَيْرٌ لِّلَّذِيْنَ يُرِيْدُوْنَ وَجْهَ اللهِ، وَأُولَئِكَ هُمُ الْمُفْلِحُوْنَ. وَمَا آتَيْتُمْ مِّنْ رِّباً لِيَرْبُوَ فِيْ أَمْوَالِ النَّاسِ فَلاَ يَرْبُوْ عِنْدَ اللهِ، وَمَا آتَيْتُمْ مِنْ زَكَاةٍ تُرِيْدُوْنَ وَجْهَ اللهِ فَأُولَئِكَ هُمُ الْمُضْعِفُوْنَ (الروم : ٣٧ - ٣٩) .

See they not that Allah expands the provision and restricts it to whomsoever He pleases? Verily, in that are signs for those who believe. So give what is due to the kindred, the needy and the wayfarer. That is best for those who seek the pleasure of Allah and it is they who will prosper. That which ye lay out for increase through the property of (other) people, will have no increase in the sight of Allah. But that which ye lay out for charity seeking the pleasure

111

of Allah (will increase): it is these [people] who will get [a recompense] multiplied (30:37-39)

Some *mufassirun* believe that this verse is not regarding *the riba* which is forbidden. This much is certain that this verse was not revealed for proscribing 'riba,' but the word 'riba' is present here, so as far as the question of the meaning of 'riba' in the *Shari'ah* is concerned, we are entitled to use this verse as an argument.

In this verse Allah has sagaciously ordered us to help kinsmen and the poor: first of all He has told that the property we have is not the result of our efforts only but is due to favourable circumstances and Allah is the creator of the causes that made our efforts successful, or because of which we got the wealth. So whatever wealth we have, in fact, belongs to Allah and it should go to those who are entitled, that is, the poor and the indigent. Those who act according to this principle are in fact benefiting themselves because in this way Allah is pleased and only Allah increases their sustenance. And those who seek profit by means of *riba*, instead of *Zakat*, they are the losers. Thus this verse also shows that *riba* and *Zakat* have one thing in common, that is, taking an increase on loans given to the indigent and the wayfarer who are allowed to receive *Zakat*, is *riba*, because *riba* and *Zakat* are compared in these Qur'anic verses.

## (b) Result of Jews' disobedience

The other verse is regarding the disobedience of Jews. *Riba* was forbidden to them but they did not obey this injunction. As a result, they were deprived of worldly luxuries, that is, worldly supremacy and the like:

فَبِظُلْمٍ مِّنَ الَّذِينَ هَادُوا حَرَّمْنَا عَلَيْهِمْ طَيِّبَاتٍ أُحِلَّتْ لَهُمْ وَبِصَدِّهِمْ عَنْ سَبِيلِ اللهِ كَثِيراً، وَّأَخْذِهِمُ الرِّبَا وَقَدْ نُهُوا عَنْهُ، وَأَكْلِهِمْ أَمْوَالَ النَّاسِ بِالْبَاطِلِ (النساء : ١٦٠ - ١٦١) .

For the iniquity of the Jews we made unlawful for them certain good things [of life] which had been lawful for

112

them, and because they hindered many from Allah's way, and because they took usury though they were forbidden, and because they devoured people's property wrongfully (4:160-161).

## (c) 'Eating property wrongfully'

What is the meaning of eating property wrongfully? A Qur'anic verse about this precedes the above verse:

يَا أَيُّهَا الَّذِينَ آمَنُوا لاَ تَأْكُلُوا أَمْوَالَكُمْ بَيْنَكُمْ بِالْبَاطِلِ إِلاَّ أَنْ تَكُونَ تِجَارَةً عَنْ تَرَاضٍ مِنْكُمْ (النساء : ٢٩) .

O ye who believe! Eat up not your property among yourselves unjustly; except if there is amongst you traffic and trade by mutual agreement.

According to the *Shari'ah, riba* is definitely an unlawful way of acquiring wealth. The above verse holds trade with mutual agreement between parties as lawful. Now, let us see what is the meaning of 'trade' and what is the criterion of 'mutual agreement.'

## (d) Meaning of 'trade'

That financial deal is called 'trade' in which someone exchanges his goods with the goods of another person. This may be in cash or on credit. Both parties seek similar benefits for themselves from this deal, and every party is equally free in this deal and is satisfied with it.

Apart from trade, there is only one other way of exchanging money with money, that is borrowing. But borrowing itself could be intended for trade, that is, with an intent to earn benefit instead of satisfying basic needs. For example, someone borrows money to buy commercial goods or to purchase land and promises to pay the creditor a little more money in addition to the original loan because he thinks that having bought the land or the goods for trade

**113**

he will have earned much more profit even after having paid the loan and interest.

Another case of borrowing is that a person is compelled to borrow in order to meet his basic needs of life survival.

In the first case, the two parties to the deal have equal status and each party makes the commitment after thorough consideration. No party has a superiority over the other, so the deal is lawful and it is considered a form of 'trade.'

In the second case, apparently there may be an agreement with the borrower's 'consent' but, in fact, one party to this agreement, the needy person, is incapable of true consent to the agreement. So if there is a commitment for an increase over the actual amount, it will be under compulsion, and such a deal will be unlawful. There is another aspect: trading cannot be done with an incapable and poor person. Being generous and meeting his needs is our religious duty. This person represents a case for benefaction. Trading in place of benefaction amounts to making a religious obligation a means to acquire worldly wealth which is unlawful and this amounts to oppression, that is, *zulm* ظلم which literally means 'placing a thing in a wrong place.'

### (e) Criterion for mutual consent

'Mutual consent' means that both parties should be satisfied with each other's terms. This word may be used only when both the parties agree equally to a deal. Consent of both sides is compulsory. Now the question is: what is the criterion for the 'consent'? I have already stated and again submit here that 'consent' has a relative meaning. If 'consent' means that someone be completely satisfied with his profit from a deal, then I would submit that it would be vain to look for such a consent in worldly people in temporal affairs. A king is not satisfied with half of the world under his rule, a trader always wants to double his profit. If an idiotic client offers a thousand *rupees*, instead of five hundred to a lawyer, will he refuse it? If a client gets a

114

lawyer free will he like to waste his money in paying his fees? So if the lawfulness and unlawfulness of deals are based on the pleasure and satisfaction of one party or the other, every case of trade will be unlawful because sometimes a trader sells an item costing ten *rupees* for twenty *rupees* and the customer buys it with pleasure. But if the same trader sells the same thing for eight *rupees* and bears a loss of two *rupees* from his pocket, will the customer not be even happier? However, all ʿ*ulama* are unanimous that if someone, due to his helplessness or for some other consideration, sells a commodity of a hundred *rupee* for *rupees* fifty only, it is permissible to buy it. Similarly, if a customer buys a commodity, costing a hundred *rupees*, for *rupees* two hundred with pleasure, then it is permissible to sell it at that price. It is obvious that if a customer buys a certain thing for double the price he does so because of his need or intense liking and if a vendor sells at a loss he too does so due to his need or for some consideration. In other words, there is need on both sides, but if the seller gets a profit, or the customer gets it free of cost, both will prefer to be benefited. So in every deal there is bound to be an element of compulsion, and there is no possibility of total satisfaction. That is why, according to law, 'satisfaction' means that the parties to the deal should be equally free in concluding the agreement, none should be under pressure, and none of the parties should be in such an abject need that in avoiding the deal he may have to risk his life. This much is enough for agreeing to a deal. For example, two persons are travelling in the African desert. One of them may not have water and may be on the verge of death, the other person has a can of water but he is prepared to give him water only if the thirsty companion sells his diamond valued at hundreds of thousands of *rupees* for a glass of water. It is obvious that he will be prepared to give his diamond in order to save his life. Will this 'deal' be considered a case of mutual consent? Certainly not. This apparent consent is not consent at all, because the need of one of the parties is so intense that he had to enter into such a deal with a heavy heart.

Now take another example: I have a piece of paper in the hand-writing of my respected teacher *Allamah* Shibli. He had written it for a very important political occasion which changed the face of the politics of Islamic India. In terms of money, this piece of paper is not worth a single *paisa* as it has already been published in several newspapers and periodicals and it is written on an ordinary piece of paper in a broken hand-writing. But it is a souvenir of my teacher and I love it. A western orientalist, who in 1878 wrote a philosophical history of the freedom movement of India, wants to buy this piece of paper due to its historic importance and wants to keep it in his library. But I am not prepared to part with this piece of paper. In desperation, the orientalist urges a n antique-loving millionaire of his country to buy it. In these circumstances, I demand at least one hundred thousand *rupees* for that piece of paper and the matter is settled after some amendments. Is this deal unlawful? Certainly not. Both the parties were free to conclude the deal. None of them was blinded by a compelling need.

Similarly, if someone borrows money for purchasing land and promises to pay interest, there is no reason why this promise to pay the interest is not regarded as to have been made with his free will simply because he would have been happier if he received it without interest. This consent will be regarded as lawful according to the *Shariʿah* because his need was not such as to divest him of the capacity to understand the nature of the deal and calculate his profit and loss. He weighs the ups and downs and considers purchase of land more profitable than the payment of interest and, therefore, agrees to the payment of interest. On the contrary, an innocent person is involved in a false case of committing homicide. He needs to borrow for paying the fees of the pleaders. In this case, if he agrees to pay interest, his commitment is not proper because his need for survival is so intense that he is unable to consider the consequences of his action.

## 31.
## Which *riba* was forbidden to the Jews

Another conclusion drawn from the foregoing verse is that the Jews were destroyed because they charged *riba* which was forbidden to them under the *Shari'ah*. So let us read the *Bible* to find out what was the deed that the Jews were forbidden to do. This will help us ascertain the meaning of *riba* in the Qur'anic sense.

## 32.
## Verses of the *Bible* regarding *riba*

(1) If thou lend money to any of <u>my people that is poor</u> by thee, thou shalt not be to him as an usurer, neither shalt thou lay upon him usury (Exodus, 22:25).

(2) And if <u>thy brother be waxen poor, and fallen in decay with thee</u>, then thou shalt relieve him: yea, though he be a stranger, or a sojourner, that he may live with thee. Take thou no usury of him, or increase: but fear thy God; that thy brother may live with thee. Thou shalt not give him thy money upon usury nor lend him thy victuals for increase (Leviticus, 25:35-7).

3. Thou shalt not lend upon usury to <u>thy brother, usury of money, usury of victuals, usury of any thing</u> that is lent upon usury. <u>Unto a stranger thou mayest lend upon usury</u> but unto thy brother thou shalt not lend upon usury: that the Lord thy God may bless thee in all that thou settest thine hand to in the land whither thou goest to possess it (Deut., 23:19-20).

117

A careful reading of these instructions of the Bible will define for us the definition of *the forbidden 'riba,'* i.e., the increase which is charged from an indigent person over and above the original loan. This increase is forbidden when taken from one's brother, that is brother-in-faith, and in the land which is under the rule of one's faith. Thus in the foregoing underlined words 'poor,' 'lend' and 'brother' occur repeatedly, and in verse no. 1 above 'my people' means Banu Israel and in no. 2 'with thee' clearly indicates that *riba* was forbidden in that land where Banu Israel ruled. The last quotation completely clarifies the matter as it allows taking of interest from strangers, and as for the purpose of this permission, it has been stated where the inheritor of the land is Banu Israel, that is, where they are ruling, they are successful there and they are blessed by God in the performance of their great deeds. Thus where does the question arise to apply such a rule to a slave community?

In addition to the Qur'anic verses mentioned earlier, there is another verse in *Surah* Al ʿImran:

يَا أَيـُّهَا الَّذِينَ آمَنُـوْا لاَ تَـأْكُلُوا الرِّبَا أَضْعَافاً مُّضَاعَفَةً (آل عمران :

١٣٠).

O ye who believe! Devour not usury, doubled and multiplied (3:130).

In this glorious verse, while double and multiplied *riba* is forbidden, permissibility of a lesser *riba* is also obvious. According to *mufassirun*, this verse was revealed before the total proscription of *riba* so that gradually it is banned totally, for in this verse double or multiplied *riba* is forbidden and there is no doubt about the total proscription of *riba*.

Now we want to ponder over those verses about which all *mufassirun* agree that they are about the total proscription of *riba*. As we shall discuss them in detail, so for the sake of providing the context the two *rukuʿs* preceding this verse are fully reproduced here:

**118**

# 33

# Two *ruku*'s on the prohibition of *riba*

يَا أَيُّهَا الَّذِينَ آمَنُوا أَنفِقُوا مِنْ طَيِّبَاتِ مَا كَسَبْتُمْ وَمِمَّا أَخْرَجْنَا لَكُمْ مِنَ الأَرْضِ، وَلَا تَيَمَّمُوا الْخَبِيثَ مِنْهُ تُنْفِقُونَ وَلَسْتُمْ بِآخِذِيهِ إِلَّا أَنْ تُغْمِضُوا فِيهِ، وَاعْلَمُوا أَنَّ اللهَ غَنِيٌّ حَمِيدٌ . الشَّيْطَانُ يَعِدُكُمُ الْفَقْرَ وَيَأْمُرُكُمْ بِالْفَحْشَاءِ، وَاللهُ يَعِدُكُمْ مَغْفِرَةً مِنْهُ وَفَضْلًا، وَاللهُ وَاسِعٌ عَلِيمٌ . يُؤْتِي الْحِكْمَةَ مَنْ يَشَاءُ، وَمَنْ يُؤْتَ الْحِكْمَةَ فَقَدْ أُوتِيَ خَيْرًا كَثِيرًا، وَمَا يَذَّكَّرُ إِلَّا أُولُوا الأَلْبَابِ . وَمَا أَنفَقْتُمْ مِنْ نَفَقَةٍ أَوْ نَذَرْتُمْ مِنْ نَذْرٍ فَإِنَّ اللهَ يَعْلَمُهُ، وَمَا لِلظَّالِمِينَ مِنْ أَنصَارٍ . إِنْ تُبْدُوا الصَّدَقَاتِ فَنِعِمَّا هِيَ، وَإِنْ تُخْفُوهَا وَتُؤْتُوهَا الْفُقَرَاءَ فَهُوَ خَيْرٌ لَكُمْ، وَيُكَفِّرُ عَنكُمْ مِنْ سَيِّئَاتِكُمْ، وَاللهُ بِمَا تَعْمَلُونَ خَبِيرٌ . لَيْسَ عَلَيْكَ هُدَاهُمْ وَلَكِنَّ اللهَ يَهْدِي مَنْ يَشَاءُ، وَمَا تُنْفِقُوا مِنْ خَيْرٍ فَلِأَنْفُسِكُمْ، وَمَا تُنْفِقُونَ إِلَّا ابْتِغَاءَ وَجْهِ اللهِ، وَمَا تُنْفِقُوا مِنْ خَيْرٍ يُوَفَّ إِلَيْكُمْ وَأَنْتُمْ لَا تُظْلَمُونَ . لِلْفُقَرَاءِ الَّذِينَ أُحْصِرُوا فِي سَبِيلِ اللهِ لَا يَسْتَطِيعُونَ ضَرْبًا فِي الأَرْضِ، يَحْسَبُهُمُ الْجَاهِلُ أَغْنِيَاءَ مِنَ التَّعَفُّفِ، تَعْرِفُهُمْ بِسِيمَاهُمْ، لَا يَسْأَلُونَ النَّاسَ إِلْحَافًا، وَمَا تُنْفِقُوا مِنْ خَيْرٍ فَإِنَّ اللهَ بِهِ عَلِيمٌ . الَّذِينَ يُنْفِقُونَ أَمْوَالَهُمْ بِاللَّيْلِ وَالنَّهَارِ سِرًّا وَعَلَانِيَةً فَلَهُمْ أَجْرُهُمْ عِنْدَ رَبِّهِمْ، وَلَا خَوْفٌ عَلَيْهِمْ وَلَا هُمْ يَحْزَنُونَ . الَّذِينَ يَأْكُلُونَ الرِّبَا لَا يَقُومُونَ إِلَّا كَمَا يَقُومُ الَّذِي يَتَخَبَّطُهُ الشَّيْطَانُ مِنَ الْمَسِّ، ذَالِكَ بِأَنَّهُمْ قَالُوا إِنَّمَا الْبَيْعُ مِثْلُ الرِّبَا، وَأَحَلَّ اللهُ الْبَيْعَ وَحَرَّمَ الرِّبَا، فَمَنْ جَاءَهُ مَوْعِظَةٌ مِنْ رَبِّهِ فَانْتَهَى فَلَهُ مَا سَلَفَ، وَأَمْرُهُ إِلَى اللهِ، وَمَنْ عَادَ فَأُولَئِكَ أَصْحَابُ النَّارِ، هُمْ فِيهَا خَالِدُونَ . يَمْحَقُ اللهُ الرِّبَا وَيُرْبِي الصَّدَقَاتِ، وَاللهُ لَا يُحِبُّ كُلَّ كَفَّارٍ أَثِيمٍ . إِنَّ الَّذِينَ آمَنُوا وَعَمِلُوا الصَّالِحَاتِ وَأَقَامُوا الصَّلَاةَ وَآتَوُا الزَّكَاةَ لَهُمْ أَجْرُهُمْ عِنْدَ رَبِّهِمْ، وَلَا خَوْفٌ عَلَيْهِمْ وَلَا هُمْ يَحْزَنُونَ . يَا أَيُّهَا الَّذِينَ آمَنُوا اتَّقُوا اللهَ وَذَرُوا مَا بَقِيَ مِنَ الرِّبَا إِنْ كُنتُمْ مُؤْمِنِينَ . فَإِنْ لَمْ تَفْعَلُوا فَأْذَنُوا بِحَرْبٍ مِنَ اللهِ وَرَسُولِهِ، وَإِنْ تُبْتُمْ فَلَكُمْ رُؤُوسُ أَمْوَالِكُمْ، لَا تَظْلِمُونَ وَلَا تُظْلَمُونَ . وَإِنْ كَانَ ذُو عُسْرَةٍ فَنَظِرَةٌ إِلَى مَيْسَرَةٍ، وَأَنْ تَصَدَّقُوا خَيْرٌ لَكُمْ إِنْ كُنتُمْ تَعْلَمُونَ . وَاتَّقُوا يَوْمًا تُرْجَعُونَ فِيهِ إِلَى

اللهِ، ثُمَّ تُوَفّى كُلُّ نَفْسٍ مَّا كَسَبَتْ وَهُمْ لاَ يُظْلَمُونَ (البقرة : ٢٦٧ – ٢٨١).

O ye who believe! Spend of the good things which ye have earned, and of the fruits of the earth which we have produced for you. And do not aim at anything which is bad, out of it ye may give away something, when ye yourselves would not accept it except with closed eyes. And know that Allah is free of all wants, and worthy of all praise. Satan threatens you with poverty and bids you to conduct unseemly. And Allah promises you His forgiveness and bounties. And Allah cares for all and He knows all things. He grants wisdom to whom He pleases; and he to whom wisdom is granted received indeed a benefit overflowing; but none will receive admonition except men of understanding. And whatever ye spend in charity of whatever vow you make, be sure Allah knows it all, but the wrong-doers have no helpers.

If ye disclose [acts of] charity, even so it is well, but if ye conceal them, and make them reach the poor, that is best for you. It will remove from you some of your [stains of] sins. And Allah is well-acquainted with what ye do. It is not for you to guide them to the right path. But Allah guides to the right path whom he pleases. Whatever of good ye spend benefits your own souls. And ye shall only spend seeking the Face [pleasure] of Allah. And whatever good you spend, shall be rendered back to you, and ye shall not be dealt with unjustly. [Charity is] for those in need, who, in Allah's cause are restricted (from travel) and cannot move about in the land. The ignorant thinks, because of their modesty, that they are free from want. Thou shalt know them by their mark: they beg not persistently from all and sundry. And whatever of good you give, be assured Allah knoweth it well.

Those who spend of their goods by night and by day, in secret and in public, [will] have their reward with their Lord: on them shall be no fear, nor shall they grieve.

Those who devour usury will not stand except like the one whom the Satan by his touch hath driven to madness. That is because they say: "Trade is like usury,' but Allah

120

has permitted trade and forbidden usury. Those who desist, after receiving admonition from their Lord, they shall be pardoned for the past; their case is for Allah [to judge]; but those who repeat [these offences] are companions of the Fire: they will abide therein [for ever]. Allah deprives usury of all blessing, but gives increase for deeds of charity: for he loveth not any ungrateful sinner.

Those who believe, and do deeds of righteousness, and establish regular prayers and give Zakat, will have their reward with their Lord: on them shall be no fear, nor shall they grieve.

O ye who believe! Fear Allah, and give up what remains of your demand for usury, if you are indeed believers. If you do it not, take notice of war from Allah and His messenger: but if you repent you shall have your capital sums: deal not unjustly, and ye shall not be dealt with unjustly. If the debtor is in a difficulty, grant him time till it is easy for him to repay, but if ye remit it by way of charity, that is best for you if ye only knew.

And fear the Day when you shall be brought back to Allah. Then shall every soul be paid what it earned. And none shall be dealt with unjustly.

Now read these verses thoroughly. You will find that prior to proscribing *riba*, two *ruku's* have been devoted to persuasion for charity and benefaction to the poor and the indigent, *i.e.*, generosity, has been mentioned as a means to attract Allah's pleasure and blessings and a way to increase wealth. The faithful have been assured that they will he repaid by Allah for their generosity and they will not be losers by spending their money for Allah's sake.

# 34

# The Third *ruku* prohibiting *riba*

After this introduction begins the third *ruku*:

يَا أَيُّهَا الَّذِينَ آمَنُوا إِذَا تَدَايَنْتُمْ بِدَيْنٍ إِلَى أَجَلٍ مُسَمَّى فَاكْتُبُوهُ، وَلْيَكْتُبْ بَيْنَكُمْ كَاتِبٌ بِالْعَدْلِ وَلَا يَأْبَ كَاتِبٌ أَنْ يَكْتُبَ كَمَا عَلَّمَهُ اللهُ فَلْيَكْتُبْ، وَلْيُمْلِلِ الَّذِي عَلَيْهِ الْحَقُّ وَلْيَتَّقِ اللهَ رَبَّهُ وَلَا يَبْخَسْ مِنْهُ شَيْئاً، فَإِنْ كَانَ الَّذِي عَلَيْهِ الْحَقُّ سَفِيهًا أَوْ ضَعِيفًا أَوْ لَا يَسْتَطِيعُ أَنْ يُمِلَّ هُوَ فَلْيُمْلِلْ وَلِيُّهُ بِالْعَدْلِ . وَاسْتَشْهِدُوا شَهِيدَيْنِ مِنْ رِجَالِكُمْ فَإِنْ لَمْ يَكُونَا رَجُلَيْنِ فَرَجُلٌ وَامْرَأَتَانِ مِمَّنْ تَرْضَوْنَ مِنَ الشُّهَدَاءِ أَنْ تَضِلَّ إِحْدَاهُمَا فَتُذَكِّرَ إِحْدَاهُمَا الْأُخْرَى . وَلَا يَأْبَ الشُّهَدَاءُ إِذَا مَا دُعُوا . وَلَا تَسْأَمُوا أَنْ تَكْتُبُوهُ صَغِيرًا أَوْ كَبِيرًا إِلَى أَجَلِهِ، ذَلِكُمْ أَقْسَطُ عِنْدَ اللهِ وَأَقْوَمُ لِلشَّهَادَةِ وَأَدْنَى أَلَّا تَرْتَابُوا إِلَّا أَنْ تَكُونَ تِجَارَةً حَاضِرَةً تُدِيرُونَهَا بَيْنَكُمْ فَلَيْسَ عَلَيْكُمْ جُنَاحٌ أَلَّا تَكْتُبُوهَا، وَأَشْهِدُوا إِذَا تَبَايَعْتُمْ. وَلَا يُضَارَّ كَاتِبٌ وَلَا شَهِيدٌ، وَإِنْ تَفْعَلُوا فَإِنَّهُ فُسُوقٌ بِكُمْ، وَاتَّقُوا اللهَ، وَيُعَلِّمُكُمُ اللهُ، وَاللهُ بِكُلِّ شَيْءٍ عَلِيمٌ (البقرة : ٢٨٢) .

O ye who believe: when you borrow from each other for a fixed period of time, register it in writing. And let a scribe write down, with justice, the transaction between you. Let not a scribe refuse to write as Allah has taught him. So let him write and let the person who incurs the liability dictate and let him fear Allah, his Lord, and let him not diminish anything from writing. If the party liable is mentally deficient or unable himself to dictate, then let his guardian dictate justly. And make two of your men witnesses. And if there are not two men [present], then a man and two women of your choice of witnesses so that if one of them errs the other reminds her. The witness should not refuse whenever they are called [to witness]. Disdain not to reduce to writing [your contract] for a future period, however small or big it may be. This is more just in the sight of Allah, more suitable for witness and more convenient to prevent doubts among yourselves, except if there is ready transaction you carry out between yourselves, then there is no blame on you if you reduce it not to writing. But take witness whenever you make a commercial transaction. And let neither scribe nor witness be harmed and if you inflict such harm it would be wickedness in you. And fear Allah, and Allah teaches you, and Allah is well-acquainted with all things (2:282).

# 35.
# The time of the third ruku‘
# and the cause of its revelation

Now let us determine the time and the circumstances of the revelation of this verse. *Sahih al-Bukhari* says in the chapter about the *ayah*: وَذَرُوا مَا بَقِيَ مِنَ الرِّبَا إِنْ كُنْتُمْ مُؤْمِنِينَ (البقرة : ٢٧٨) (And give up what remains of your demand for usury, if ye are indeed believers – 2:278) that Ibn ‘Abbas said:

آخر آية نزلت على النبي صلى الله عليه وسلم آية الربا (صحيح البخاري ، كتاب التفسير ، سورة البقرة ، باب ”واتقوا يوما ترجعون فيه الى الله“ ، فتح الباري ، ج ٨ ، ص ١٦٤)

The last verse revealed to the Prophet, *pbuh*, was the verse on *riba*.

You have already read ‘Umar's report quoted in *Musnad Ahmad* where he said that ‘the last part of the Qur'an revealed is the verse of *riba*; the Prophet, *pbuh*, died without interpreting it to us, so avoid *riba* and doubtful (dealings)’:

إن آخر ما نزل من القرآن آية الربا وإن رسول الله صلى الله عليه وسلم قبض ولم يفسرها فدعوا الربا والرية (مسند أحمد، مسند عمر بن الخطاب ، ج ١، ص ٦٠) .

123

In his *khutbah* of *Hajjat al-Wida* (the Last, or the Farewell, Pilgrimage), the Prophet *(pbuh)* said:

وربا الجاهلية موضوع، وأول ربا أضعه ربانا : ربا العباس بـن عبدالمطلب فإنه كله موضوع (صحيح مسلم ، كتاب الحج ، رقم الحديث ١٤٧ ، ج ١ ، ص ٨٨٩ ؛ وبكلمات متقاربة فى أبي داؤد ، كتاب المناسك ، باب صفة حجة النبي صلعم ، رقم الحديث ١٩٠٥ ، ج ٢ ، ص ١٨٥ ، وابن ماجة ، كتاب المناسك ، رقم الحديث ٣٠٧٤ ، ج ٢ ، ص ١٠٢٥ ، وسنن الدارمي ، كتاب البيوع ، رقم الحديث ٢٥٣٤، ج ٢ ، ص ١٩٨).

The first *riba* that is abolished is our *riba*: *riba* of [my uncle] Al-*Abbas ibn *Abd al-Muttalib. It wholly stands abolished.

From this it is clearly proved that this verse was revealed *after* the conquest of Makkah and the first *riba* abolished in accordance with this *shar'i* rule occurred *after* Makkah had been conquered and Islamic administration was established in Arabia. If there remains any doubt about it that too is cleared from the *Tafsir* of *Imam* al-Razi:

في سبب نزول الآية روايات : الرواية الأولى أنها خطاب لأهل مكة كانوا يرابون، فلما أسلموا عند فتح مكة أمرهم الله تعالى أن يأخذوا رؤوس أموالهم دون الزيادة (التفسير الكبير، ج ٧، ص ٨٧) .

There are several narrations about the circumstances for the revelation of this verse. The first is that it is addressed to the people of Makkah who indulged in *riba* transactions. When they embraced Islam after the conquest of Makkah, Allah ordered them to take back their [original] capital and forego the extra amount.

124

## 36.
## Some narrations
## about the cause of the verse's revelation

There are several narrations in this respect. The first one is
that it is addressed to the people of Makkah who did usury
business. When they embraced Islam at the time of the
conquest of Makkah, they were ordered to forego excess
money and be satisfied with the original amounts lent by
them.

Now let us see what sort of transaction was called 'riba'
by Arabs and what was the nature of *the riba* forbidden by
this verse. In other words, what were the circumstances of
the revelation of the verse. You have already read what
Imam Baghawi, in his *Tafsir Ma'alim al-tanzil*, has stated
with reference to the narrations by 'Ata and 'Ikramah,
about the circumstances of the revelation of this verse.
*Imam al-Razi* also says the same thing in his *al-Tafsir al-
Kabir*:

والرواية الثالثة : نزلت في العباس وعثمـان بن عفـان رضـي الله
عنهما، وكانا أسلفا في التمر، فلما حضر الجذاذ قبضـا بعضـا، وزادا
في الباقي فنزلت الآية . وهذا قول عطاء وعكرمة . والرواية الرابعـة:
نزلت في العباس وخالد بن الوليد وكانا يسـلفان في الربا (التفسـير
الكبير، ج ٧، ص ٨٧).

The third narration is that this verse was revealed
regarding al-'Abbas and 'Uthman ibn 'Affan, for both of
them dealt in advance purchase of dates. At the time of
harvest they used to take part of their purchase and
increase the quantity of the remaining part. Therefore, this
verse was revealed. This is the statement of 'Ata and
'Ikramah.

The fourth narration is that it was revealed about Al-
'Abbas and Khalid ibn al-Walid, for both of them dealt in
advance purchase of dates.

In any case, all narrators agree that the verse was revealed
about Al-'Abbas, and this is understood from the Prophet's

(*pbuh*) *khutbah* that after the proscription of *riba*, Al-ʿAbbas was the first person to adhere to this rule after the conquest of Makkah.

Now what was the form of the deals Al-ʿAbbas used to have in Makkah? According to al-Baghawi and al-Razi, his deals were a kind of *bayʿ salaf*, that is they used to pay the price of the dates crop in advance (in cash or in kind). At the time of the deal there used to be no agreement for an increase as is indicated from the details narrated by Baghawi.

When the dates harvest was ready, many debtors were unable to repay all that was due, for if they gave away all, they would not be left with what was necessary for their own survival. Under compulsion, they repaid part of the dues and promised to repay the balance with an increase for a grace period until the next crop.

That this verse is related to *bayʿ salaf* is apparent from the very words of the *ayah*:[32]

فَمَنْ جَاءَهُ مَوْعِظَةٌ مِّنْ رَّبِّهِ فَانْتَهَى فَلَهُ مَا سَلَفَ (البقرة : ٢٧٥) .

Those, who after receiving admonition from their Lord, desist, shall be pardoned for <u>the past</u> (2:275).

This is further supported by the verses following the verse on *riba*. The *rukuʿ* referred to above is followed by this verse:

يَا أَيُّهَا الَّذِينَ آمَنُوا إِذَا تَدَايَنْتُمْ بِدَيْنٍ إِلَى أَجَلٍ مُّسَمًّى فَاكْتُبُوهُ (البقرة : ٢٨٢) .

O ye who believe: when you borrow from each other for a fixed period of time, register it in writing.

*Imam* al-Razi, in his *al-Tafsir al-Kabir*, has mentioned about this verse the words of *Imamul mufassirin* Ibn ʿAbbas:

إنها نزلت في السلف (الرازي ، التفسير الكبير ، ج ٧ ، ٩٤) .

It is revealed about credit trading.

---

[32] It uses the Arabic word '*salaf*' whose meaning is underlined in the English translation (ed.)

Thus the time of revelation, the circumstances of revelation and the context of the wordings of the Qur'an itself as well as the *khutbah* of the Prophet (*pbuh*) prove the following assertions.

# 37.
# Conclusions of the foregoing discussion and their non-applicability in India

(1) The *riba* forbidden according to the Qur'anic verse is regarding *bay<sup>c</sup> salaf*.

(2) The people forbidden to indulge in *riba* dealings were all Muslims.

(3) The country where *riba* was forbidden had Islamic administration and the proscribing verse was not revealed until Islamic administration was established.

Are these conditions applicable to the interest/*sood*-based dealings in India? Certainly not. Neither the practice of *bay<sup>c</sup> salaf* is common today, nor is there the concept of imposing one-sided conditions in the event of the borrower's failure to repay after the expiry of the fixed period. And even if such an agreement for interest is made today one can get a decree from a court of law, for that agreement would be under duress and in the circumstances of helplessness and distress, the pressure would be unlawful and it will be regarded as an 'unconscionable bargain' in legal terminology.

Moreover, in India neither do we have our own government nor are our dealings restricted to Muslims alone. Thus it is clear that the present-day interest-based

127

business neither comes under *riba* nor are the *fiqhi* injunctions applicable to it. Neither is it proved to be unlawful in the light of the *Hadith* or the Qur'an.

It may be said here that the circumstances of revelation do not invest any speciality into a general rule, so justification on the strength of the circumstances of the verse's revelation is wrong. I would submit that, no doubt, rules derived from the Qur'anic verses are not limited to the circumstances of their revelation. But this only means that the injunctions of a verse are not limited to a particular individual or event regarding which the verse was originally revealed and that injunction will be applicable to all events and persons under similar circumstances. But this generality does not mean that the injunction will still be applicable where the nature of the matter is not similar nor such conditions prevail in accordance to which some injunction had been revealed.

To sum it up, if the case for the proscription of *riba* can be argued with reference to the Qur'anic text, it is only when the nature of the case is that of *bayᶜ salaf*, parties to the deal are Muslims and the place of the deal is *Dar al-Islam*.

## 38.
## The course of action in the absence of a clear definition of *riba*

While there is no definition of *riba* in the Holy Qur'an and the *Hadith*, and while it is agreed that *every* increase is not forbidden, we are compelled to adopt one of the two courses to determine the meaning of '*riba*.'

128

## (a) Tradition of the Arabs

In the first course, the definite article in *al-riba* (*the riba*), denotes *familiarity, i.e., the riba* forbidden in the verse is the one which was known and prevalent among Arabs at the time. For this purpose the prevalent practices among Arabs will have to be studied and the kinds of dealings targeted by the verse in question identified, and those dealings will have to be considered as *the forbidden riba*.

A close examination shows that the only dealing of this kind prevalent among the Arabs was *bay' salaf.* There is no evidence that Arabs practised any interest-based trade dealings of the kind prevalent today. So if the Arab practices are to be relied upon for determining the meaning of *'the riba'* and the interpretation of the verse, the only conclusion will be the one that has already been submitted.

## (b) Inference (*qiyas*) and its details

The second course is to analyse the details of the particular dealing, about which the proscription has been revealed, in order to see what the intent of the *Shari'ah* is by that rule and thus a general rule is inferred and that rule is applied wherever those circumstances prevail. This is called 'inference' (*qiyas*) which is the fourth among the four arguments of the *Shari'ah*.[33] This general rule will not be the final one but in the midst of the world's ever-changing developments there is no way out except to rely on inference.

Now, for the sake of arriving at the right inference, the following points will have to be considered:
(1) What general rule can be deduced by the event that was the cause of the revelation of that order?

---

[33] The other three are: the Divine Revelation (Qur'an), *Hadith* (sayings or deeds of the Prophet (*pbuh*)) and *ijma'* (consensus) of Islamic scholars (ed.).

(2) Is it supported or not by Qur'anic verses, by their internal relationship as a whole and by the context?

(3) Is there any moral or social consideration implied in this principle or not?

(4) Whether any other Qur'anic verse or a clear saying or act of the Prophet (*pbuh*) contradicts it or not and whether the deduced general rule is not clearly against rationality?

## 39.
## Advance purchase of crops by Al-ᶜAbbas

Now take the incident that was the cause of the revelation of the verse. According to the explanation by *Imam* Al-Baghawi, the nature of the incident is as follows:

كان العباس وعثمان بن عفان يشتريان التمر بالدفع المقدم (معالم
التنزيل، ج ١، ص ٣٨٩ ، ط. دار الكتب العلمية، بيروت ، مع تفسير الخازن)

Al-ᶜAbbas and ᶜUthman ibn ᶜAffan used to buy dates by advance payment.

Al-ᶜAbbas [and ᶜUthman ibn ᶜAffan] used to make advance dealings in dates, that is, he [/they] used to pay the owner of trees the price of his forthcoming crop in advance. It is not clearly mentioned in the *hadith* whether the price thus paid was in cash or in the shape of dates or any other grain. Probably it was not a cash dealing, rather dates or grains were given because only those poor would sell their crops in advance who were starving without food. Otherwise why should they sell in advance?

However, as the details are not specified in the *hadith*, we can concede both the cases [cash or kind payment].

When the dates ripened, the owner would say: if you take away your due, that is, the whole crop of dates, my children will starve, so take some dates and give me time to pay the rest till the next harvest.

This incident indicates that such deals were made with the poor and starving persons. In these circumstances they used to agree to pay the remaining quantity of dates in double quantity at the next harvest. The same would be repeated again at the next harvest for the trees were the same trees. Thus the balance would never be paid up.

## 40.
# Inference of some *ulama*
## from the order regarding advance purchase

Some *ulama* deduce the following principle from the incident:

لو أقرضنا مالاً يباع بالكيل والوزن وتكون به طَعَمية وثَمَنية حسب قول الإمام الشافعي ، وذلك لمدة معينة، ثم لو استعدنا المال من نفس الجنس بعد انقضاء المدة فأي مبلغ إضافي زائد على رأس المال الأصلي، والذي يؤخذ كعوض على مدة الاستعمال، هو من الربا .

If we lend someone for some time a commodity which is sold by weight and measure, and according to *Imam* Shafi'i it has edibility and price-value; and if, after the expiry of the appointed period, at the time of repayment we take back same commodity in kind, in that case the excess amount charged for the extended period of utilisation will be *riba*.

Is this inference correct? Certainly not.

## 41.
# Rational reasons for my disagreement
# with the said inference by ᶜulama

My reasons are as follows:
1.  The condition of the exchange of commodity-with-commodity in this inference is not proved by the wordings of the *hadith*, because therein there is no specification about the charge for the advance purchase.
2.  While deducing this principle, many details of the facts have been overlooked although those very details are the reasons for the order rationally and according to narrations. They are as follows:
    *(a)*  A poor and helpless person, unable to repay the previous due, used to agree to pay an excess. In the case of the repayment of the whole amount of the due he would not be able to sustain himself and his family. In this state of helplessness he was unable to conclude a deal with his creditor freely, neither would his 'consent' be really considered as true. In the terminology of the *Shariᶜah*, this is called *bayᶜ al-mudtarr* بيع المضطر (sale or deal of the desperate) which is unlawful. To quote ᶜAli,

    وقد نهى النبي صلى الله عليه وسلم عن بيع المضطر  (أبو داؤد، رقم الحديث ٣٣٨٢، ج ٣، ص ٢٥٥) .

    The Prophet, *pbuh*, prohibited the sale/deal of the desperate.

    *(b)*  There used to be no pre-condition for an increase at the time of making the deal, which would have provided the borrower with an early opportunity to reject such a deal.
    *(c)*  The place of the order was *Dar al-Islam*.
    *(d)*  Both the creditor and the borrower were Muslims and were subjects of the Islamic administration.

3.  This inference goes against the dealings of the Prophet (*pbuh*) himself and against his orders, because in similar

132

circumstances he gave two camels in return for one, and said that the best one of you is the one who repays his debt in the best way.

4. This inference is clearly against rationality for the following reasons:

(a) There is no reason why a person, who is the owner of his wealth, should be compelled to forgo the charges for the use of his money in every incidence and in dealings with *everybody*.

(b) The *Shariʿah* has permitted exactly similar cases. For example, if a house is purchased using the same money, rent can be collected. If a horse or a camel is bought, a charge can be levied for its use. If a piece of land is purchased it can be given on rent. Now, if it is argued that in these cases the use and the profit is definite and that it is not so in the case of a loan, then I would submit that both cases are similar. A tenant may use the house or keep it vacant, yet he will have to pay the rent after having signed the agreement. Similarly a cultivator may cultivate the land or leave it fallow, the land owner will not be responsible for it. Under the *Shariʿah*, the land-owner remains entitled to receive the rent for his land. Then, in the case of a commodity or money being lent, why should not the creditor get a charge for the use of his commodity or money without any consideration for whether any profit was made or not by the borrower?

(c) Having no consideration for the status/ circumstances of the persons involved in a deal and the place of the deal is also against rationality.

(d) As there is no incentive for giving loans, this order may be interpreted as prohibition of offering credit, while business cannot continue in this world without credit and mutual cooperation.

(e) If this inference is taken to be correct, no moral, cultural or social exigency is detected in this rule.

133

Our 'ulama have gone to great lengths to rationalise this rule. The reasons they state are summarised as follows:

5.1 *Riba* is exchange of money against an appointed period of grace for repayment مبادلة الأموال بالآجال , that is, the [excess] money is taken as a charge for the *time* allowed. Time is a relative issue and it is not the property of the creditor. Therefore, the extra money collected by the creditor, as a charge for the *time* allowed, is in fact in lieu of nothing on the part of the creditor. The weakness of this explanation is obvious for the following reasons:

(a) This case is applicable to only *bay' salaf* referred to above because in its case a charge for the benefit from the borrowed commodity/money was not determined at the time of making the deal and only later a commitment for an increase was forced on the debtor against allowing him more time for repaying the due. Here there is no doubt about the unlawfulness of the *bay' salaf*-type of transactions mentioned above.

(b) The premise that 'interest' is the charge for *time* is wrong altogether. Rather, it is the charge for the *benefit* drawn by the debtor from the commodity/money of the creditor and for the sacrifice that the creditor undertakes by depriving himself of the benefits of his property. However, the quantity of the benefit and sacrifice is naturally fixed according to the period of time allowed. So the 'interest' is never without a charge. No doubt the charge for the commodity/money is not in the form of commodity/money. Instead, it is for the presence/absence of commodity/money and for the pleasure/pain caused by its presence/absence to the two parties to the deal.[34]

---

[34] The borrower is pleased by getting someone's money and the creditor is pained by parting with his money and apprehension about its repayment on time (ed.).

134

The case of service is similar. When someone does something for me he takes some trouble on the one hand and, on the other, he gives me some rest or pleasure, so I pay him a charge for that service. Similarly, when I give my land to someone on rent, on the one hand, I deprive myself of the benefits I would expect from that land and, on the other hand, the cultivator gets an opportunity to work and he expects every possible benefit to accrue from someone else's property during the period of cultivation. The charge for this benefit is called rent. My land might have been unutilized or I might not have used it for my own benefit or might not want to use it in future. Similarly, it is quite likely that the cultivator may not reap any benefit to compensate him for the rent he paid or the hard work he put in, due to a natural calamity, and he may even have to bear the cost of the seeds from his pocket. Still the cultivator will have to pay the rent for the whole period of time the land remains with him. And when I will re-take possession of my land from the cultivator not a single iota of it would be left with him. So is this rent also without a charge?

Just as I am not the master of time, I do not own the clouds, air, the sun and the moon that help growth, but just as my land is a source of probable benefit for the cultivator and I get a charge for it in the form of rent, in the same way I am the owner of the *rupee* I possess and I should get a charge for those benefits and pleasures that could be obtained through that *rupee*.

The difference in these two cases is said to be that in the case of a debt the actual money is used up and in the case of rent of house or land, the land or the house remain as they were. In the first place this difference is not so great as to forbid the taking of the charge in one case and make it permissible in the second case. Secondly, where is the difference in the two cases? Both the cases are

135

exactly similar, for the ownership is not transferred in any of the two cases. Just as the landlord continues to be the owner of his land, similarly the owner of the *rupee* or a certain quantity of 'value' remains the creditor and so he is entitled to receive his due. Just as the right to use the land is temporarily transferred to the cultivator, the debtor acquires the right to benefit from the value of the borrowed money. Neither the land is used up nor the loan is lost because the loan is not the name of a *rupee*, guinea or a currency note but it is the name of that *value* or *purchasing power* which is the cause of that loan and which is temporarily transferred from the creditor to the debtor.

5.2 The second explanation about the proscription of *riba* is as follows in the words of *Imam* al-Razi:

قال بعضهم : الله تعالى إنما حرم الربا من حيث إنه يمنع الناس عن الاشتغال بالمكاسب، وذلك لأن صاحب الدرهم إذا تمكن بواسطة عقد الربا من تحصيل الدرهم الزائد، نقدا كان أو نسيئة، خف عليه اكتساب وجه المعيشة ، فلا يكاد يحتمل مشقة الكسب والتجارة والصناعات الشاقة، وذلك يفضي الى انقطاع منافع الخلق . ومن المعلوم أن مصالح العالم لا تنتظم إلا بالتجارات والحرف والصناعات والعمارات (التفسير الكبير، دار الكتب العلمية ، بيروت ، ١٩٩٠، ج ٧ ، ص ٧٧).

Some people have said that Allah made *riba* unlawful because it prevents people from engaging in useful occupations. This is because the wealthy, being able to earn the extra *dirham* through *riba*, whether in cash transactions or through credit dealings, will have little trouble in earning his livelihood and will not put in effort to earn his bread or engage in trade or difficult occupations. This will result in the miscarriage of public interests. It is well-known that the world's interests are not taken care of except through trades, occupations, industry and construction works.

In his book on economics, Walker has made the same objection. Apparently this objection seems to be very wise but its mistakes are evident for the following reasons:

(a) This purpose [making people earn their bread with hard work] cannot be achieved by the mere proscription of *riba*, unless and until Man is deprived of the right of ownership of inheritance and his earnings [savings].

(b) Suppose a person, instead of lending his money on interest, rents out his landed property, inherited or purchased by his own earnings. Is this, again, not that same situation where a capitalist enjoys life while remaining idle? Thus you can see that today not the *mahajan* (money-lender) but the landlords and *zamindars* are unnecessary elements of the society. Then why is one thing permissible and the other forbidden?

(c) If one is entitled to benefit from his capital, there is no reason why he should not charge others for the right to use that benefit.

(d) What is the use of proscribing *riba* alone, unless lending too is made mandatory? Because when the capitalist cannot get any benefit out of his loaned money, why should he lend his money to anyone in the first place? This one-sided order is useless and the consideration that has been mentioned to justify it is mere logical deception.

5.3 The third reason put forward is the theory that profit in the form of 'interest' is *fixed* and, therefore, it is not permissible.

The answer to this assertion is that the 'rule' that 'fixed profit' is unlawful is a mere invention of someone which has no basis in the *Shari'ah*. There is no such principle in The Book [Qur'an] and the *Sunnah* of the Prophet, *pbuh*. And is not the rent on land a fixed profit? In this case, too, is there not the possibility of both profit and loss for the cultivator? Then why is it permissible for you to take a fixed amount from the cultivator?

5.4 The fourth reason put forward is that without any consideration for pecuniary benefit every person has a moral duty to help his brother-in-need, to satisfy his want and not to charge any price for performing this moral duty.

In other words, this means that a rich person has no right to make unlawful profit from the distress of a poor and needy person. Moreover, if a member of our society is falling into the precipice of destruction due to his poverty, to save him from that destruction and make him a useful element is beneficial for society as a whole and the creditor is also indirectly benefited from his generosity. This reason is certainly rational and if the order forbidding *riba* was revealed due to this reason then this order of the Sustainer of the universe exactly conforms to His Sustainership. However, if this is the only reason for the proscription of *riba*, then the following matters should be specified:

*(a)*   The meaning of 'need' must be defined.

*(b)*   The purpose of the loan should be specified.

*(c)*   As this order is a social one, the relationship of the two parties should be taken into consideration, that is, benefaction should not be obligatory for the enemy or the rival, and the decision about enmity or rivalry should not be made in the light of an individual's relations but from a collective point of view affecting the whole community of Muslims.

*(d)*   Similarly, as these matters are related to society, the place of their application should be where Islamic laws prevail.

Now let us see how far these factors have been taken into consideration in the fore-mentioned definition. I would submit that none of this has been taken into consideration. My reasons are as follows:

(a) Making *riba* conditional on commodity-for-commodity, weight and measure does away with the very purpose of the rule and opens the way for all kinds of piracy.

(b) In the above-mentioned inference the status of the debtor, his relationship with the creditor, the nature of his need and the purpose of the debt, have not been taken into consideration. The rich and the poor, the landlord and the trader, the king and the beggar, all have been treated equally. Similarly, a loan taken for survival, or for touring India in a motor car, or for establishing a railway company, all have been treated on an equal footing. The people who are entitled to our benefaction have not been given any preference. So if the aim of the *Shari'ah* by this rule is to deny the rich any opportunity to exploit the needy poor, the definition of *riba* should not be what *fuqaha* have mentioned.

(c) The political status of the debtor and his relationship with the creditor have not been taken into consideration in this definition. If the *Shari'ah* permits killing of a person in certain circumstances then why *riba*, which is much inferior to taking someone's life, has not been made permissible with some persons?

6. Does the context of the Qur'anic verses support this inference? Not at all.

# 42

# The inference of the author

You have seen the objections to the forgoing inference. Now let us make our inference about the same case, keeping in view all the details, and test it according to the same criteria.

Our inference is as follows: if a poor person, who is entitled to take *sadaqat* [charity], takes a loan to sustain himself or his family; or a debtor who is unable to pay his dues and in the case of paying back his dues he will not be left with enough money to maintain his family, enters into an agreement for an increase over the amount due or on the actual loan, this is an agreement of *riba* which is unlawful. But this non-permissibility is conditional on two factors:

(a) the place where this agreement is made should be under Islamic rule, that is where the government's orders are issued according to the intent of the *Shari'ah* even in financial matters.

(b) The transaction should be between Muslims and if either of the parties is a non-Muslim, he should at least enjoy rights equal to that of Muslims, that is, he should be a *dhimmi*.

## 43.
# Reasons for my inference
# in the light of the Islamic sources

It is apparent that there can be no rational objection to this definition. Now, let us see whether our inference is correct or not in the light of traditional sources of the Shari'ah.

First of all, take the case of 'Abbas' bay' salaf about which a revealed text exists. Our forgoing definition of riba covers all details of this event and entails no superfluous and extraneous conditions like commodity-for-commodity. The poverty of the debtor is evident from his pleading that 'if you take away your dues nothing will be left for my children to eat.'[35]

The criterion of 'need' mentioned by us is that the person is entitled to receive sadaqah: this too is proved by the incident in question, for the quantity of dates in the hands of the indebted person is already sold to another person in advance, so at present he is completely insolvent; whatever he is keeping back for his children is somebody else's property, so it is proper for him to receive sadaqah.

The condition that the purpose of loan should be survival of life is also present in this case, because the quantity of dates he holds back from his debtor is like a loan which he takes for the sustenance of his family.

Now take the conditions/circumstances. The rule on riba is revealed after the conquest of Makkah when the Islamic administration, according to the directions of the Prophet (pbuh), was extended to Makkah and the parties to the deal are all Muslims.

The only remaining question is that in our inference riba dealing with a dhimmi is stated to be unlawful in our definition. Here there was no case of a dhimmi. The reason for this is merely this: dhimmis and Muslims have similar rights and they have been included due to this assumption

---

[35] See page 97 above.

as it has been accepted in *fiqh* that the sanctity of a *dhimmi's* property is like the sanctity of his life (حرمة ماله كحرمة دمه).

Thus this inference is completely applicable to the event in the text referred to. Now, let us see if any *hadith* or any dictum of the *Shariʿah* contradicts this definition? None! Rather, with this definition certain contradictions are removed which arise *vis-à-vis* the proscription of *riba* and some incidents like the borrowing of one camel for two and land rent are clarified.

## 44.
## Our claim supported
## by the verse proscribing *riba*

Now let us see whether our inference is supported by the verse proscribing *riba* or not? In this respect I do not have to say much. The whole *rukuʿ*, preceding the *rukuʿ* which contains the *ayah* on *riba*, is devoted to persuading people to spend in the Way of Allah. It is an eloquent sermon on the religious and moral obligation to give *sadaqah* and help the poor. Moreover, another verse regarding *riba* in *Surah al-Rum* is also preceded by the instruction where *riba* has been compared with *Zakat*:

فَآتِ ذَا الْقُرْبَى حَقَّهُ وَالْمِسْكِينَ وَابْنَ السَّبِيلِ (الروم : ٣٨) .

So give the due to the relative, the poor and the wayfarer (30:38).

Does this not clearly prove that *riba*-based loan and *sadaqah* have a common purpose: that is meeting the basic wants of a needy person. And the criterion of this 'need' is that the

142

poor may not have any thing for his sustenance. Thus the context of the Qur'anic verses confirms the meaning of *riba* as stated by us.

## 45.
## Studying the verse forbidding *riba*

Now let us study the verse on *riba* and see the outcome. The first piece of the verse proscribing *riba* is as follows:

الَّذِيْنَ يَأْكُلُوْنَ الرِّبَا لاَ يَقُوْمُوْنَ إِلاَّ كَمَا يَقُوْمُ الَّذِيْ يَتَخَبَّطُهُ الشَّيْطَانُ مِنَ الْمَسِّ، ذَلِكَ بِأَنَّهُمْ قَالُوْا إِنَّمَا الْبَيْعُ مِثْلُ الرِّبَا (البقرة : ٢٧٥) .

Those who devour usury will not stand except as stands one whom Satan by his touch hath driven to madness; that is because they say: 'Trade is like usury' (2:275).

*Riba*-eaters, *i.e.*, people who charge *riba*, have been compared to the person under trance and devoid of his senses, or he is warned to be treated like this on Doomsday. The reason for this in the words of the Holy Qur'an is that these people say that *riba* and *bay*ᶜ are transactions of the same kind. In other words, in spite of their apparent similarity, the two types of deals are, in essence and as a matter of principle, different from each other.

Now let us see what is the common feature on the basis of which *riba*-eaters say that both are similar and what is that important difference, for overlooking which, Allah calls them devoid of their senses.

As I have already stated earlier, all kinds of monetary/financial deals are called *bay*ᶜ except those borrowings which a man undertakes for the purpose of sustaining himself. For example: exchange of commodity is

143

*bay<sup>c</sup> muratalah*, exchange of coins is *bay<sup>c</sup> sarf* and advance purchase is called *bay<sup>c</sup> salaf*. In *surah* Jumu ah this word, *bay<sup>c</sup>*, has been used in this wider sense:

فَاسْعَوْا إِلَى ذِكْرِ اللهِ وَذَرُوا الْبَيْعَ (الجمعة : ٩) .

So hasten earnestly to the remembrance of Alláh, and leave all business.

## 46.
## Similarity between loans and *bay<sup>c</sup>*

Now let us see what is the similarity between loan and *bay<sup>c</sup>* and what is the difference between them. The similarity is obvious that the trading of commodities is common to them both. A trader takes a profit over the actual price of his commodity and a money-lender demands interest for his money. Then what is the difference? The difference is very important.

In the trading of goods, both parties are equally in need. So whether the trader makes a profit or suffers a loss or the buyer gets things costing ten *rupees* for *rupees* twenty or *rupees* eight the parties are really free to strike the deal. But there is a world of difference between a needy borrower and a carefree money-lender. On the one hand there is a need that blinds the foresight of the borrower and on the other hand there is the selfish and carefree money-lender exploiting this need. Similarly, in the case of *bay<sup>c</sup> salaf*, on the one side there is a demanding and satisfied lender who is legally entitled to receive his due when the appointed period is over and on the other side there is a helpless debtor. If he pays back the debt he intentionally plunges into the hell of starvation, so if there is any agreement about an increase over the original amount of the debt it will certainly be one-sided. This is the difference which cannot be overlooked. And on this very basis Allah says:

وَأَحَلَّ اللهُ الْبَيْعَ وَحَرَّمَ الرِّبَا (البقرة : ٢٧٥) .

And Allah allowed trade and forbade *riba* (2:275).

Now, if the traditional definition of *riba* is accepted, there is no difference between *bay*ᶜ and *riba*, because the debt, which is not intended to save life, and where the borrower is not incapable, is in no way different from *bay*ᶜ. For example, an aristocrat takes a fancy to a horse for no valid reason. A trader had bought this horse for a paltry sum of *rupees* two hundred. Now the aristocrat is hell-bent on acquiring that horse to satisfy his whim. The trader reads the emotions of the aristocrat. First of all, he shows his unwillingness to sell the horse, but at last demands one thousand *rupees* for the horse and the aristocrat pays with pleasure. Thus the trader exploits the aristocrat's indulgence and charges five times the original price. Similarly, there is a landowner, whose partner sells his share and an enemy buys it with a view to take revenge only. Now the landlord is compelled to use his right of pre-emption in order to save his land from the partnership of an enemy. He has some cash and for the balance he cannot manage without a loan. Being under the impression that the acquisition of his land is more comfortable for his life than the payment of interest, he borrows on interest. The landlord is neither starving nor is he a pauper; rather, he owns property worth millions and if he parts with even a piece of his land he can get double the amount of loan, but parting with his land is a matter of dishonour for him. On the contrary, he wants to acquire more land with a view to make a profit, to remain respectable in his society and to earn more prestige. Now, the money-lender comes to know of these feelings of the landlord and knows that there is no real need and that there is no religious or worldly benefit in giving an interest-free loan to such a well-to-do person, and demands a fixed charge for the right to benefit from his money, then what is wrong about his doing so? The trader and the moneylender both benefit by their goods. Both are benefited by the

145

intensity of the desire of their partners and both the partners to the agreements are well-to-do persons. Then why is one of them held to be a sinner and the other is taken as innocent? Thus the case under discussion will have to be excluded from *riba* and it will have to be made compulsory condition for *riba* that the borrowing party is in real need because that can be the only difference between *bay* and *riba*. This is confirmed by the following verses.

# 47.
## *Riba* and *sadaqah* compared

يَمْحَقُ اللهُ الرِّبا وَيُرْبِي الصَّدَقَاتِ (سورة البقرة : ٢٧٦) .

Allah deprives usury of all blessing, but gives increase for deeds of charity (2:276).

Here *sadaqah* and *riba* have been compared. This too indicates that both have the same place and occasion. Because if someone says that I like *Moong khichri* [an Indian food] very much and I like *kumayt* horse very much, the listener is sure to think that he is crazy. The horse is used for riding and *khichri* is a food: what is the comparison between them? Similarly, when *riba* as a cause of loss and *sadaqahs* as a cause of prosperity are mentioned together, this statement will be taken to be reasonable only when their circumstances are the same. If taking *riba* from every rich and poor is unlawful then how can it be compared with *sadaqah* ? *Sadaqah* is meant for the poor and the indigent only. When the circumstances of the two acts are different, the comparison between them is meaningless.

In fact there are only three ways of meeting the basic wants of the needy.

First of all, whatever is given to them to enable them to satisfy their need is all waived and the matter left to Allah to reward. This is called *sadaqah*. *Zakat* is obligatory but if one comes across a poor person after having paid his/her *zakat*, there is scope to give *sadaqah* which is a virtuous act, though not obligatory.

The second method is that whatever is given to the needy is offered as *qard hasan* [good loan]. It means that the person presently in need will be bound to return that loan without any increase when he is capable of repaying it, and at that time if he repays a little more to the creditor, of his own free will, it will not matter, rather it is a virtuous act. But as the deal was made at a time when the indebted person was in dire need and there was no stipulated increase so the creditor will be entitled to receive the actual amount only. This is the case of *qard hasan*. Meeting the wants of a needy Muslim should be obligatory at least in this way for every well-to-do Muslim. The Holy Qur'an orders in the imperative form: (وَأَقْرِضُوا اللّٰهَ قَرْضًا حَسَنًا (المزمل : ٢٠) (and lend to Allah good loan — 73:20). The use of the imperative verb implies it to be obligatory.

The third way to meet the need is to compel the needy person to pay more than the actual loan. This third method is called 'riba' which is forbidden, and it is, in fact, the exact opposite of the second method.

In effect, the intent of the *Shari'ah* is that the need of the poor must be met somehow or the other. If *sadaqah* is given, nothing like it: it is an all in all virtue. But everybody cannot be so generous as to wash his hands off his wealth. Similarly, there may be many self-respecting poor who do not like to accept *sadaqah* or those who are not permitted to accept it such as the *sadat*.[36] Then how should the need of such people be met? Taking the general human nature into consideration, it has been ordered that if you cannot give *sadaqah* or the poor person is not in a position to accept it, then you must give him *qard hasan* and meet his needs in some way or the other but do not put the condition of increase on repayment. The first case is *mustahabb* (commendable), the second one is *wajib* (obligatory) and the third is *haram* (forbidden), while the occasion of all the three is the same: to meet the need of the needy.

# 49.
## Obligation of *qard hasan*

Some people describe 'interest' as forbidden on the one hand, but on the other, do not regard *qard hasan* as obligatory (*wajib*). Rationally, as well as a matter of justice, the proscription of one and the obligation of the other are inter-related. Rationally, because the proscription of *riba* is in fact the opposite of the order whose positive side is: وَأَقْرِضُوا اللّٰهَ قَرْضاً حَسَناً (المزمل : ٢٠) (and lend to Allah the good loan – 73:20). So if the negative aspect is forbidden, the positive aspect must be obligatory.

To be just, you may say that if *riba* is forbidden and there is no obligation to lend, the consequences will be worse. In such circumstances many people may die of

---

36 Sadat سادات (pronounced *saadaat*), pl. of *sayyid*, are the descendants of the Prophet (*pbuh*), through his daughter Fatimah and cousin and son-in-law, ᶜAli ibn Abi Talib (**ed.**).

starvation or, being helpless, may borrow from others and then be destroyed and cause a collective loss to the community and some feeble-minded persons may even be forced to change their religion. Yet the well-to-do Muslims will neither give an interest-based loan, due to the proscription of *riba* in the Qur'an, nor feel bound by the *Shari'ah* to give *qard hasan*. Thus they escape the sin of *riba* only to commit a worse sin indirectly. Still, according to the religious precepts, they are not held responsible.

However, *qard hasan* being obligatory is clearly evident. Now, if *qard hasan* is obligatory, it must be for the poor and indigent. What is the sense in making it obligatory for buying a motor car or for touring Europe?

## 50.
## Explanation of the verse 2:279

Now if *qard hasan* is made obligatory only to alleviate the hardships of the poor, then the proscription of *riba* will also be applicable to dealings with them. And the criterion of being 'poor' in the *Shari'ah* is a person's entitlement to receive *sadaqah*. This argument of ours is further supported by the following verses:

وَإِنْ تُبْتُمْ فَلَكُمْ رُؤُوسُ أَمْوَالِكُمْ، لاَ تَظْلِمُوْنَ وَلاَ تُظْلَمُوْنَ (البقـرة : ٢٧٩).

But if ye repent ye shall have your capital sums: deal not unjustly, and ye shall not be dealt with unjustly (2:279).

Literary taste suggests that here [in وَلَا تُظْلَمُونَ] we have *waw haliyah* (واو حالية).[37] And the reason for لا تَظْلِمُونَ (deal not unjustly) has been expressed by ولا تُظْلَمُونَ (and ye shall not be dealt with unjustly). Otherwise the condition of being oppressed is a result of action of others and occurs as a compulsion, so what is the sense in its negation?

*Imam* al-Razi has explained it as follows:

أي لا تَظْلِمُون الغريم بطلب الزيادة على الرأسمال ولا تُظْلَمُون أي
بنقصان الرأسمال (التفسير الكبير ، دار الكتب العلمية، بيروت ، ط: ١ ،
١٩٩٠ ، ج ٧ ، ص ٨٨).

Do not wrong the debtor by asking him to pay more than the original sum due; and you will not be wronged, means that you will not be paid less than the original sum.

Literary considerations apart, this explanation is rationally beguiling. Suppose a rich person due to the consideration of monetary profit pays back a little more to his creditor, what injustice has been done to him, especially when the Prophet(*pbuh*) himself did so, and said:

خياركم أحسنكم قضاءً (صحيح البخاري ، كتاب الاستقراض ، باب حسن
القضاء، فتح الباري ، ج ٥ ، ص ٤٥ ؛ وفى صحيح مسلم ، كتاب المساقاة ، باب من
استلف شيئا فقضى خيرا منه ، رقم الحديث ١٢١ ج ٢ ، ص ١٢٢٥ : "خياركم
محاسنكم قضاءً") .

The best of you are the best of you in the repayment of debts.

However, if a poor person is compelled to agree to a *riba* agreement, forcing him to fulfil that agreement is injustice. Arabic lexicons explain ظلم (injustice) as placing something in a wrong place (وضع الشئ فى غير محله). A poor person does not have the power to make an agreement in the first place. So an oppressive agreement is, in fact, injustice to him. In other words, it is 'placing something in a wrong place.' Such an agreement cannot be enforced legally. Moreover, a

---

[37] *I.e.*, it denotes time and state. In other words, the *ayah* says: deal not unjustly *while* you are not dealt with unjustly (ed.).

needy person is entitled to beneficence rather than profiteering from.

## 51.
## Need is a necessary condition for *riba*

In the light of the foregoing discussion, need is the necessary condition for the occurrence of *riba*. As we proceed, this becomes clearer. Allah says:

وَإِنْ كَانَ ذُوْ عُسْرَةٍ فَنَظِرَةٌ إِلَىٰ مَيْسَرَةٍ، وَأَنْ تَصَدَّقُوْا خَيْرٌ لَّكُمْ (البقرة : ٢٨٠)

If the debtor is in a difficulty, grant him time till it is easy for him to repay, but if ye remit it by way of charity, that is best for you (2:280).

This noble verse was revealed after the Conquest of Makkah on the occasion of the Farewell Pilgrimage, *Hajjatul wada*, and it has instructions about past *riba* dealings. The *riba* dealings at that time were all *bay salaf* transactions. In *bay salaf* there used to be no pre-determination of *riba* at the time of the original agreement. When the borrower, because of his poverty, was unable to repay on time, he prayed for some more time and was compelled to agree to an increase over the actual due.

151

# 52

# Revelation of the verse for relinquishing *riba*

For the above-mentioned reasons, when this verse was revealed after Islamic rule had been established over Arabia, whatever excess amounts over the actual loans had already been received by the creditors, according to earlier agreements, were left with them but the remaining amounts of *riba* under the agreement were abolished:

وَذَرُوا مَا بَقِيَ مِنَ الرِّبَا (البقرة : ٢٧٨)

And give up what remains of your demand for usury (2:278).

Although there may have been creditors who had already received double or four times the actual loan, they were not ordered to return the excess money they had already taken nor was the paid up amount deducted from the actual loan. The actual loan was still held to be due for payment. Only the balance of *riba* was waived, and the *riba* received earlier, before the introduction of Islamic rule, was exempted. At the time of proscription no new agreements of loan were taking place. Instead, payments were being made only for the existing agreements. So the rich borrowers were ordered to repay the actual due and consider themselves free from the liability of the unlawful agreement for *riba* they had to make when they were in need. But with regard to those borrowers who were not yet able to repay the actual due, the creditors were instructed to grant them time till it was easy for them to repay, and if they (creditors) relinquish the claim to the original loan by way of charity that was the best for them. This shows that those entitled to such leave in time are the persons in need. And the criterion for being 'needy' is that *sadaqah* could be lawfully given to him:

وأن تصدقوا خير لكم إن كنتم تعلمون (البقرة : ٢٨٠)

[But] if you remit it by way of charity that is best for you, if you only knew.

This verse also clears the point that it is not lawful for rich Muslims to be in debt. This is the reason why there is no instruction to give a grace period to such persons. And it is evident from *ahadith* that the Prophet (*pbuh*) did not perform the funeral prayers of persons who died in debt. This also clarifies the point that loans taken by rich people for luxury, trade or for any other unnecessary purpose, are not 'loans' in terms of the *Shariʿah*. Instead such dealings are a kind of *mudarabah* (trade partnership) or *ikra'* (lease/rent). The existence of a *sharʿi* need is the foremost condition for 'loan.'

# 53.
## Our inference about *riba*

Our conclusion is that *riba* is the conditional increase in the amount of loan given to a poor person entitled to receive *sadaqah* in order to meet his needs without being subject to conditions of commodity or measure or weight. This inference is proved, to a credible extent, by the Qur'anic verses, their context and the circumstances of their revelation.

Now let us see whether the conditions of *Dar al-Islam* and that of being a Muslim for *riba* to apply, are also proved by the Holy Qur'an or not. We have already seen the verses in *Surah al-Baqarah*. We considered the first part of لَا تَظْلِمُونَ وَلَا تُظْلَمُونَ (deal not unjustly, and ye shall not be dealt with unjustly – 2:279) from a different aspect. Now consider وَلَا تُظْلَمُونَ (and ye shall not be dealt with unjustly). There is no sense if it is taken to mean that 'you receive the actual sum so no injustice is done to you.' This is because if the creditor gets back only his actual sum, having left it in someone else's custody for a period of time, he is a loser anyway. Had he been ordered to give in *sadaqah* (charity) even the original sum, what injustice would have befallen him? The creditor was rich and *sadaqah* is a cause for God's blessing.

When we delve deeply into وَلَا تُظْلَمُونَ (and ye shall not be dealt with unjustly), the meaning emerges that there is no possibility of injustice to you also. That is, being in an Islamic State if tomorrow, God forbid, you are in need of a loan, no body can demand *riba* from you. However, *mufassirun* have not derived this meaning and no new meaning, however right it may be, can be acceptable, so we do not want to be satisfied with this argument only.

# 54.
## Jews and Muslims have the same *riba*

*Riba* was definitely forbidden for Jews. No Qura'nic verse shows that the *riba* forbidden by the Islamic *Shariʿah* is different from that of the *Shariʿah* of Moses. Rather, we discover that the same *riba* is forbidden in both *Shariʿahs*. Thus says Allah:

فَبِظُلْمٍ مِّنَ الَّذِينَ هَادُوا حَرَّمْنَا عَلَيْهِمْ طَيِّبَاتٍ أُحِلَّتْ لَهُمْ وَبِصَدِّهِمْ عَنْ سَبِيلِ اللهِ كَثِيرًا، وَأَخْذِهِمُ الرِّبَا وَقَدْ نُهُوا عَنْهُ (النساء : ١٦٠ – ١٦١) .

For the iniquity of the Jews We made unlawful for them certain good [things] which had been lawful for them; and because they very much hindered from Allah's

154

Way; and because they took usury, though they were forbidden, and because they devoured people's wealth wrongfully (4:160-161).

The same idea has been expressed thus in the *Bible:*

If thou lend money to any of <u>my people that is poor</u> by thee, thou shalt not be to him as an usurer, neither shalt thou lay upon him usury (Exodus, 22:25).

And if <u>thy brother be waxen poor, and fallen in decay with thee</u>, then thou shalt relieve him: yea, though he be a stranger, or a sojourner, that he may live with thee. Take thou no usury of him, or increase: but fear thy God; that thy brother may live with thee. Thou shalt not give him thy money upon usury nor lend him thy victuals for increase (Leviticus, 25:35-7).

In other words, the first condition for the occurrence of *riba* is that the borrower should be indigent just as mentioned in our definition of *riba.*

Secondly, the creditor and the borrower should be brothers (كل المؤمنين إخوة 'all believers [in Islam] are brothers').

Thirdly, for the occurrence of *riba* it is necessary that it must be 'amongst yourselves,' that is, where you have your government, *i.e.,* in *Dar al-Islam.* This condition has been fully clarified by the following verse of the *Bible:*

Thou shalt not lend upon usury to <u>thy brother, usury of money, usury of victuals, usury of any thing</u> that is lent upon usury. <u>Unto a stranger thou mayest lend upon usury</u> but unto thy brother thou shalt not lend upon usury: that the Lord thy God may bless thee in all that thou settest thine hand to in the land whither thou goest to possess it (Deut., 23:19-20).

# 55

# The reason for restricting the application of the rule of *riba to Dar al-Islam*

...................................................................................................

After this elucidation in the *Bible*, there is no scope for any doubt for the enlightened that both *the riba* forbidden to Banu Israel and the one proscribed for Muslims in the Holy Qur'an are subject to the condition that it must occur within an Islamic State, the persons involved must be Muslims, and if they are non-Muslims they should be those that have equal rights with Muslims such as *dhimmis*. Rationally and justifiably this is what should be the case. The reasons for this, in short, are as follows:

### (a)
### Community's benefit through individual help

The order forbidding *riba* is a social law. Through this law one person is compelled to treat another person kindly and to make financial beneficence to him.

First of all, there should necessarily be a distinction of status, especially in a natural religion like Islam which gives priority to relatives even in *sadaqat*.

Now, if this order is equally applicable to relatives and strangers, then, apart from being unnatural, it will deprive the relatives of their rights.

It is evident from the Qur'anic verses that benefaction is obligatory among Muslims only. For example:

وَلَا تَنسَوُا الفَضْلَ بَيْنَكُمْ (البقرة : ٢٣٧)

And do not forget generosity between yourselves (2:237).

وَلَا تَأْكُلُوا أَمْوَالَكُمْ بَيْنَكُمْ بِالْبَاطِلِ (البقرة : ١٨٨)

And do not eat up your property among yourselves for vanities (2:188).

Obviously, 'among yourselves' بينكم is addressed to Muslims alone.

Secondly, such laws must be obligatory for both sides:

هَلْ جَزَاءُ الْإِحْسَانِ إِلَّا الْإِحْسَانُ (الرحمن : ٦٠)

Is there any reward for good other than good? (55:60).

If this was not the case, the very intent of the order will be compromised. If we are ordered in an Islamic State that we should not contribute in the destruction of a needy member of our faith by charging *riba* from him, then it is understood that the security of the community depends upon the security of all its individual members. Thus our self-sacrifice results in an indirect benefit in the form of a flourishing community.

Moreover, due to this self-sacrifice we are ourselves not exposed to self-destruction, because, God forbid, if due to changing times we are compelled to borrow, the creditor, bound by the law of the *Shari'ah* as we are, will be obliged to do the same self-sacrifice for us. But if it is binding on us in a territory where our financial laws are not in force and we are compelled to do beneficence to people who are not bound to do beneficence to us; not only this but collectively, as a people, they are at loggerheads with us in order to gain political and economic superiority over us as a community... In such circumstances not only the intent of the order is extinguished, rather acting upon such an injunction will be tantamount to communal suicide.

Islam is not one of those religions who impart the unnatural precept that if someone slaps you on one cheek offer him the other cheek for another slap. Islam has clear instruction:

وَإِنْ عَاقَبْتُمْ فَعَاقِبُوا بِمِثْلِ مَا عُوقِبْتُمْ بِهِ (النحل : ١٢٦)

And if ye punish, let your punishment be proportionate to the wrong that has been done to you (16:126).

Islam is a living religion that promises its followers leadership and superiority in every respect:

وَأَنْتُمُ الْأَعْلَوْنَ إِنْ كُنْتُمْ مُؤْمِنِينَ (آل عمران : ١٣٩)

You are the supreme if you are faithful (3:139).

Islam teaches its followers to strive for this cause with every possible effort:

وَجَاهِدُوا بِأَمْوَالِكُمْ وَأَنْفُسِكُمْ فِي سَبِيلِ اللهِ (التوبة : ٤١)

157

> And strive and struggle, with your properties and your
> persons, in the cause of Allah (9:41).

Making efforts for the collective progress of the Muslim
*Ummah* is, in fact, an effort in the path of Allah which can
be made with life and property or both.

The world itself is an arena for struggle to survive. Not
only individuals but communities and nations as a whole
are engaged in the struggle for survival. Each nation is
struggling against other nations. This 'war' is not necessarily
done with the help of weapons but it continues in the state
of peace as well. In our time the war is mostly economic.
Islam, too, has not restricted *Jihad* for the sake of Allah to
fighting militarily only. Instead, every effort for the
superiority and dominance of the *Ummah* is *Jihad*, political
or economic or otherwise. Now if in this *Jihad* for our
people we strengthen the arms of our adversary and hand
over our weapons to him for our own destruction, is it not
treachery against our own people and can a sagacious
religion like Islam allow this?

Some people retort, if the dog bites your leg you cannot
bite him in retaliation. How can a condemnable act be
proper for the purpose of retaliation? But this argument is
not correct. Some acts are condemnable in themselves, such
as drinking, eating pork, theft etc. But they too are
permissible in certain circumstances. Some acts are neither
condemnable nor commendable in themselves; only their
place and occasion make them condemnable or
commendable. The same act, if it happens within the
permissible limits, is *Sunnah*, otherwise it is liable to death
by stoning. Social instructions are mostly of this type. The
same thing applies in the case of *riba*. Taking a charge for
the use of one's money is not condemnable in itself, but
whenever it is contrary to our moral and national duty it is
certainly condemnable. At this one may say that if Lala
Naththu Mal has extracted interest from Mir Husayn ᶜAli,
how can this entitle ᶜAbdullah Khan to take interest from
Ram Charan Singh? This has been addressed partially in the
foregoing submissions. The fact remains that it is not the
matter of individuals but that of *community*. Social or

economic agreements are made between nations rather than between individuals. Similarly, a declaration of war is made between nations and not between individuals. The soldier in the battlefield does not see whether the soldier of the opposing nation has done any personal harm to him or to his brother during the war. Every German caught in British territory during the World War was a prisoner of the British government irrespective of the fact whether that German himself had opposed the British government in any way or not. If it comes to be known that a member of our community cannot be safe from another community, then we too have the right to treat the member of that community in the same way as the members of that community could/would do to a member of our community. When this principle prevails in the matters of killing and withholding freedom according to Islam and in all civilized countries of the world, then there is no reason why the same principle should not be applied in the matter of receiving a charge for the money loaned.

## (b)
## The Connection of *riba* with business

Yet another, and the greatest, reason for making the prohibition of *riba* restricted to *Dar al-Islam* is that it is related to business which may not necessarily be between Muslims alone. Any order cannot be applicable unless the parties are bound by the same law. Moreover, power and authority are necessary for enforcing and implementing financial and social orders. This is the reason why this order was revealed towards the end of a twenty-three year-long period of the Prophethood and at a time when Makkah had been conquered and Islamic regime had been firmly established in Arabia, as if nature was waiting for the most favourable time without which the order prohibiting *riba* could not have been enforced. Is there still any doubt about the veracity of the *hadith*: لا ربا بين المسلم والحربي فى دار الحرب (there is no *riba* between a Muslim and a *harbi* in *Dar al-harb*)?

159

## 56.
## Mak-hul's narration is correct
## according to rationality and justice

Mak-hul مكحول , the narrator of the above *hadith* [that there is no *riba* in *Dar al-harb*] is a *faqih* and narrator regarded as authentic by Hanafis. For some *muhaddithun* to call him as *mudallis* مدلس (confuser),[38] is neither a divine revelation nor a Prophet's (*pbuh*) saying which we would be bound to believe. May be *muhaddithun* misunderstood Mak-hul. They were not infallible and were likely to make a mistake. Moreover, it is not necessary that narrations by a 'confuser' are always wrong and an authentic narrator's statement be always correct. Just as a truthful person may speak untruth due to some misunderstanding, similarly a liar may speak the truth. The criterion for ascertaining correctness is not only the opinion of distinguished authors of the biographical works on narrators, but the internal meaning of a particular narration itself can, to an extent, vouch for its correctness. So apart from the fact of who the narrator is of a certain narration, why not take it as the saying of the Prophet (*pbuh*) if its meaning concurs with rationality and justice and while it is supported by the orders in a revealed book, *i.e.,* the *Bible* and the circumstances of the revelation of the Qur'anic verse about *riba*. A great majority of the *Ummah,* that is the followers of the Hanafi *fiqh,* fully agree and accept this narration as correct and binding. Whatever be the debate, it is about the explanation/interpretation of *Dar al-harb.* Moreover, apart from the fact that this *hadith,* as narrated, may or may not be correct, we have to see that in a non-Muslim State which legalizes interest, is it lawful or not for a Muslim to take interest from a non-Muslim, and whether there are other arguments under the *Shari'ah* apart from this *hadith*?

---

[38] *Mudallis* مدلس is a narrator who narrates [even one *hadith* in his career] on the authority of someone he has not met or heard from *directly* (ed.).

But before proceeding any further in this discussion, I would like to narrate some interesting anecdotes to make amends for the dull academic debate so far.

## Anecdote 1

A learned friend of ours narrates the following in his typical style in contradiction of the narration by Mak-hul al-Shami:

It is said that *Hadrat* ᶜAbbas, may Allah bless him, returned to Makkah after embracing Islam and was <u>secretly</u> conducting his usury-based lending business. Although Makkah was a *dar harb* <u>at that time</u>, the Prophet (*pbuh*) abolished all his pending usury dues with the people of Arabia and said:

كل ربا كان في الجاهلية فهو موضوع وأول ربا وُضِع هو ربا العباس.

All *riba* of the *Jahiliyah* days is abolished and the first *riba* abolished is that of Al-ᶜAbbas.

Read this passage carefully. You will discover how much venomous are the two underlined pieces. One does not know whether the words 'secretly' is the invention of the writer himself or any precursor has been bestowed with this honour. The writer has, intentionally or unintentionally, not referred to any source or narrator so that the person committing this slander against Al-ᶜAbbas could be identified. However, the question arises whether at *that* time prohibition of *riba* had been revealed or not when Makkah was still a *dar harb* where Al-ᶜAbbas was doing his usury-based business? If the answer is in the negative, as the writer must be aware of, why should Al-ᶜAbbas have kept his usury deals secret? What should he be afraid of? Islam had not yet forbidden *riba* and it was not a matter of disgrace during the days of *Jahiliyah*. The people of Makkah were themselves in that kind of business. Had it been forbidden under the *Shariᶜah* by that time, then, God forbid, whether the Prophet's (*pbuh*) uncle was like a present-day 'saint' or preacher of the type who in the words of Hafiz-e Shirazi:

161

چوں بخلوت می روند آں کار دیگر می کنند

When they go to their privacy, they do something else.

Moreover, had the proscription of *riba* been revealed
earlier, it would have been enforced and many people
would have given up *riba*. Then why should the Prophet
(*pbuh*) have said in his Farewell Pilgrimage *khutbah*: ربا أول
يوضع هو ربا العباس (the first *riba* abolished is the *riba* of Al-
ʿAbbas).

Is it still not clear to the enlightened that the word
'secretly' is just an invention of a person for strengthening
his argument? But alas! This invention is also in vain. In
spite of this slander against Al-ʿAbbas, it does not contradict
Mak-hul al-Shami neither does it prove that taking *riba* is
forbidden even from a non-Muslim in *Dar al-harb*. This
would have been possible only when it could be proved
that when Al-ʿAbbas's *riba* was abolished Makkah was not
a *dar Islam* or that the people whose *riba* was waived were
non-Muslims. Probably to prove this, the writer has said
that *at that time* Makkah was a *dar harb* so that the reader is
made to understand that at the time of the abolition of *riba*
Makkah was a *dar harb*, although the writer knows it
perfectly well that the fact is contrary to this. Who else may
know better than our writer, who quoted this, that the
words كل ربا كان في الجاهلية فهو موضوع (all *riba* of the *Jahiliyah*
days is abolished) are a part of the *khutbah* delivered by the
Prophet (*pbuh*) in Makkah after its conquest and by that
time all the people of Makkah had embraced Islam. So has
the writer made a blatantly incorrect statement only to
prove his point? Only he can answer this question. In our
humble opinion, he has used the words 'at that time'
intentionally as a mark of his intellectual prowess and the
argument is so ambiguous that superficial and ordinary
readers will believe that at the time of the prohibition of
*riba* Makkah was a *dar harb* and they will submit to that
argument. But if, God forbid, a knowledgeable person
happens to see this article and raises an objection then
instantly a different stand will be taken and it will be stated
that 'that time' does not mean the time when the
prohibition of *riba* was ordered; rather, it means the time

162

when Al-ʿAbbas began his usury business when Makkah was most certainly a *dar harb*. But in that case what would happen to the argument? This will rather support the narration by Mak-hul al-Shami instead of contradicting it, because Al-ʿAbbas was charging *riba* till Makkah was a *dar harb* and the remaining *riba* was cancelled *after* Makkah became a *dar Islam*. Apart from Mak-hul al-Shami's narration, is this event alone not sufficient to prove the lawfulness of *riba* in *Dar al-harb*?

But he still has the last arrow in his quiver. He may change the whole argument of his ambiguous writing like the Persian Professor who, in spite of the objection by his pupil, insisted that خوشه چین (Persian for recipient of benefaction) may also mean the tufted tail of a fox! Similarly, he may say that his writing means that the *riba* that was due in *dar al-harb* was also abolished, whereas had it been lawful in *dar al-harb* why should the *riba* due prior to the establishment of *dar al-Islam* be abolished? This argument is easier than the previous one, for the Holy Qur'an says: وَذَرُوْا مَا بَقِيَ مِنَ الرِّبَا (give up whatever remained of the *riba* — 2:278). This shows that part of the *riba* had already been received earlier. The Holy Qur'an goes on to say: فَلَكُمْ رُؤُوْسُ اَمْوَالِكُمْ (and you are entitled to receive back your actual sums — 2:279).

This means that the *riba* received prior to the establishment of the *dar al-Islam* was held lawful and was not deducted from the principal. However, after the establishment of the Islamic regime a Muslim cannot take *riba* from another Muslim. So the remaining *riba* was abolished, that too only when Makkah became *dar al-Islam*. But whatever amount of *riba* had already been taken prior to the establishment of the Islamic State and the Makkans' embracing of Islam was held lawful, because, if held unlawful, it would have been deducted from the original loan. Thus this argument also supports Mak-hul's narration and does not contradict it. Probably our *Mawlana* wants to support *riba* in *dar al-harb* behind the veil of rejection. This view is further supported by another statement of the *Mawlana*. First of all, he has discussed in detail in his article those *ahadith* from which some *fuqaha'* derive the definition of *riba* and describe it as the explanation and elucidation of the brief Qur'anic verses.

But at long last a word of truth in the whole article impulsively trickles down from the *Mawlana*'s pen: 'Historically I fail to understand why the *hadith* explained the last verse on *riba* prior to its revelation?' It is surprising that the *Mawlana* had a difficulty in understanding it whereas prior to the revelation of the last verse regarding *riba* Al-ᶜAbbas, apprehensive of the revelation of the verse, was doing *riba* business *secretly* in Makkah, and while, according to the *Mawlana*, prior to the revelation of the verse, the Prophet (*pbuh*), as a prelude to the revelation of the verse, had already forbidden *riba* on the occasion of the Conquest of Khaybar!

## Anecdote 2

In this continuity let us narrate another joke of the *Mawlana*. In the same article about the proscription of *riba* he says:

> The most important question is whether all cases are specific with Muslims or if other peoples are also included? But a narration in *Sahih Muslim* indicates that Islam has not made any distinction in this respect. Thus the words of the *hadith* are as follows:

عن فضالة بن عبيد ، قال: كنا مع رسول الله صلى الله عليه وسلم يوم خيبر نبايع اليهود الوُقية الذهبَ بالدينارين والثلاثة، فقـال رسـول الله صلى الله عليـه وسـلم : لا تبيعـوا الذهـب بالذهب إلا وزنا بوزن (صحيح مسلم ، كتاب المساقاة ، رقم الحديث ٩١، ج ٢، ص ١٢١٤).

> Fudalah ibn ᶜUbayd says that we were with the Prophet (*pbuh*) on the day of the conquest of Khaybar and we were selling an *uqiyah* of gold to Jews for two or three *dinars*. The Prophet (*pbuh*) said: 'Do not sell gold except for an equal weight.'

The question that the *Mawlana* considers as 'the most important' is neither a question nor is its answer lies in this *hadith*. The question is not whether such deals may be made with non-Muslims or not. Instead, the question is whether taking *riba* in a country which is not under Islamic rule, and from a non-Muslim who is not a *dhimmi*, lawful or not? So you have taken out all the important elements of that question, *i.e., riba, dar al-harb* and *harbi,* and instead of *riba* you have used the words 'in this respect' and did not allow *dar al-harb* and *dar al-Islam to* creep into your question, and instead of *'harbi,'* you have expanded it by using the expression 'other peoples.' Now what importance is left in this question that you have taken the trouble to answer?

Now look at the curious answer! According to the *Mawlana* himself, the proscription of *riba* had not been revealed at the time of the conquest of Khaybar, and the *hadith* he uses for the argument does not contain the word *'riba.'* Even according to its nature, the incident itself has nothing to do with *riba*. The fact of the matter is that Muslim *mujahidun* were throwing away to the Jews their booty of gold, that is, an *uqiyah* of gold, forty *dirhams* in weight, was being sold for two or three *dinars,* which was huge loss to Muslim property. The reason for forbidding it was obvious. Then what is the sense in using this incident as an argument for the lawfulness or unlawfulness of *riba*? Moreover, the incident occurred *after* the conquest of Khaybar when Khaybar had become a *dar Islam* and the Jews, with whom the dealings were being made, were *dhimmi* subjects of the Muslim State. Is it that the *Mawlana*, behind the veil of this argument, intends to justify *riba* in *dar al-harb*?

# 57

# Definition of *Dar al-harb* and *harbi*

After these anecdotes, let us turn to the main debate. The definitions of *Dar al-harb* and *harbi* will be explained in the following pages.

Unfortunately the words *Dar al-harb* and *harbi* are such that the listener is instantly alarmed. The word 'harb' gives an idea of 'war.' But the word, in fact, is not so very horrifying. Just as war and fighting do not necessarily mean killing and blood-letting, they indicate all sorts of struggles, for example:

جنگ هفتاد ودو ملت همه را عذر بند

چوں ندیدند حقیقت ره افسانه زدند

The seventy two fighting groups are hell-bent to find excuses to fight; when they did not find truth, they took to imagination to fabricate excuses.

Or as the Urdu poet, Dagh داغ, said:

جهكي ذرا چشم جنگجو بهي، نكل گئي دل كي آرزو بهي

بڑا مزا اس ملاپ كا هے جو صلح هو جائے جنگ هو كر

The quarrelsome eye bent a little,
the heart's desire was also fulfilled
The meeting is very pleasant
when there is peace after fighting.

Similarly, in Arabic the word 'harb' حرب does not mean fighting or war only, it is used to mean opposition and struggle as well. Even in the Holy Qur'an the verses forbidding *riba* include the following:

فَأْذَنُوْا بِحَرْبٍ مِّنَ اللهِ وَرَسُوْلِهِ (البقرة : ٢٧٩)

So take notice of war from Allah and His Messenger (2:279).

Can the sword be wielded before Allah? Obviously the word 'harb' has not been used to mean war or blood-letting: *harb* means disobeying the orders of Allah and inviting His displeasure and the breaking down of the relationship that should exist between Allah and His servants.

Another cause of misunderstanding about this word is a general misconception among Muslims that it is obligatory for Muslims in a *dar harb* to either migrate (*hijrah*) or wage *Jihad'* under the leadership of an *Amir*, although such injunctions are not applicable to all kinds of *Dar al-harb*. These rules apply only to such *dar harbs* where lives of Muslims are not safe and where Muslims are forcibly restrained from performing their religious duties or where Muslim religious rites are banned under government orders.

The word *'Dar al-harb'* is, in fact, opposite *to 'Dar al-Islam.'* Where there is no Islamic rule it is a *dar harb*.

Islamic rule means where the administration is run according to Islamic tenets. Therefore, *fuqaha* have defined *dar al-harb* as: كل بلد لا يحكم فيه بحكم الإسلام (every country not administered by the rules of Islam). So a country, where the rules are not in confirmation with the rules of the *Shariᶜah*, will be a *dar harb* whether it is ruled by a Muslim or happens to be under a non-Muslim administration. However, these *dar harbs* vary in categories. If a non-Muslim state has a peace agreement with the Muslims then, according to the terms of the agreement, the rules of *dar al-harb* will be applicable there too; just as there was the kingdom of Abyssinia during the times of the Prophet (*pbuh*), where the life and property of Muslims was safe to the extent that *riba* could not be taken from Muslims under the terms of the agreement. So the Muslims too did not take *riba* from non-Muslims there. But in the absence of an agreement, as was the case of Makkah after the Truce of Hudaybiyah and before the Conquest of Makkah, taking *riba* from non-Muslims there would be permissible. If there is an actual war situation and the life and property of Muslims is unsafe, as was the case before the Truce of Hudaybiyah, then either emigration (*hijrah*) will be obligatory or if circumstances permit, its Muslims will have to go to *Jihad* under the leadership of an *Amir*.

Now, let us see in which category India falls. No doubt, there is no threat to our lives from the government, we are allowed to offer our prayers. In certain cases, such as, marriage, divorce, inheritance and *hibah* (gift), Muslims are governed according to Islamic laws. So this is not the type of *Dar al-harb* where *Jihad* is obligatory or from where emigration (*hijrah*) is required. Here fighting and quarrelling is forbidden instead of being obligatory, because it will hinder public peace and such behaviour is forbidden by the Qur'an:

وَلاَ تُفْسِدُوا فِي الأَرْضِ بَعْدَ إِصْلاَحِهَا (الأعراف : ٥٦).

And do not make mischief on the earth, after it hath been set in order (7:56).

But as far as the financial matters are concerned, is there any scope for doubt about India being a *dar harb*? No, certainly not. Are un-Islamic practices not openly common here? Are financial matters not dealt with totally contrary to Islamic laws? Whether decrees for *riba* are not issued against Muslims and the money is forcibly extracted from them? Whether after usurping possession for twelve years the ownership rights of the original owner are not forfeited and transferred to a successful usurper? Whether drinking liquor and debauchery are not openly allowed? Then what is short of India's being a *dar harb*? First of all, according to all *Imams*, it is not necessary for being a *dar harb* that all the three conditions are found at the same time.

According to the two *Imams* [Abu Yusuf and Muhammad], for a land to become a *dar harb* it is sufficient that infidel practices prevail in it openly and freely. The three requirements according to the Greatest *Imam* [Abu Hanifah] are as follows:

أولا : ألا يحكم فيها بحكم الإسلام.

ثانيا : ألا تكون متصلة بدارالإسلام.

ثالثا : ألا يبقى فيها مسلم أو ذمي آمنا بأمانه الأول الذي كان ثابتا قبل استعلاء الكفار .

(الشيباني ، كتاب السير الكبير ، حيدرآباد الدكن ، ١٣٣٥هـ / ١٩١٦ ، ج ٤ ، ص ٣٠٢ ؛ قاضيخان ، فتاوى قاضيخان (على حاشية الفتاوى العالمكيرية ، بولاق ، ١٣١٠ هـ / ١٨٩٢ ، ج ٣ ، ص ٥٨٤ ؛ السرخسي ، المبسوط ، بيروت ١٤٠٦ هـ / ١٩٨٦ ، ج ١٠ ، ص ١١٤ ؛ الكاساني ، البدائع والصنائع ، القاهرة ، ١٣٢٨ / ١٩١٠ ، ج ٨ ، ص ١٣٠).

| *Firstly:* | Islamic rules are not enforced there; |
|---|---|
| *Secondly:* | It should not be adjacent to the *Dar al-Islam*, and, |
| *Thirdly:* | Any Muslim or a *dhimmi* living there no longer enjoys the original security he enjoyed prior to the land's occupation by non-Muslims. |

I would like to argue that the *Imam* [Abu Hanifah] did not mean that all the three requirements should be found at the same time. Rather, the requirements (mentioned above by him) are in an order of priority. However, the first condition is definitely prevailing in India and except some places bordering Afghanistan, the second condition also applies to the whole of remaining India.[39]

As for the remaining third condition that too becomes evident after thorough deliberation. It is obvious that after the demise of the Islamic state there is no question of the presence of a *dhimmi*, Muslims themselves do not enjoy the same security that they had under the Islamic rule. For example, there are many acts that could be done fearlessly under an Islamic regime, such as, participation in the wars fought by other Islamic countries. But today it is such a great crime that it is punishable with life imprisonment at the least. Similarly in an Islamic regime *riba* could not be extracted from us even if any number of documents were signed by us. Not to say of twelve years, our rights could not lapse even in thousands of years as a result of unlawful usurpation by someone. Our right to property was safe even after thousands of years of usurping occupation. But today it is not. Thus we certainly do not enjoy the original security we had in the past.

The following *fatwa* in *Mawlana* ʿAbdul Hayy Firangi-Mahalli's collection of *fatawa* (vol. 2, p. 107) fully supports our view:

سوال : در عملداري نصاري اهل اسلام مبالغ نزد نصاريٰ جمع
مي سازند وسود آن از نصاري مـي گـيرند وآن را وثيقـﮧ
مي نامند درست است يا نه ؟

---

[39] This was the situation when this book first appeared in 1936 (ed.).

جواب: در دار الحرب میان مسلم و کافر حربی معامله‌ی ربا درست است بنا بر مذهبَ صاحبَین به سببِ آن که شعائر کفر بے دغدغه باعلان رواج گرفته دار الحرب است . وبنا بر مذهب امام اعظمؓ دار الاسلام که دار الحرب مي شود مشروط است به شروطِ ثلاثة بر تقدیر تحقق شروط ثلاثة در عملداري نصارى البته دار الحرب خواهد شد .

*Question:* Under Christian administration, people [followers] of Islam deposit their money with Christians and take *riba* against it from the Christians and call it *wathiqah* [bond]. Is it correct or not?

*Answer:* In *Dar al-harb*, *riba* dealing is permissible between a Muslim and a non-believer. The reason, according to the two *Imams* [Abu Yusuf and Muhammad], is that un-Islamic rules are freely enforced there and, therefore, that country is a *dar harb*. According to the *maslak* of the Greatest *Imam* [Abu Hanifah], a territory turns from a *dar Islam* into a *dar harb* if the three conditions are found there. If these three conditions are found in the territory under the Christians, that territory becomes a *dar harb*.

Now, the question remains: are Muslims obliged to deal with non-Muslims according to the rules of Islam in the kind of *dar al-harb* India happens to be where the life, faith and religious practices of Muslims are not threatened, but in financial matters neither Muslims are governed according to Islamic law nor the government has any agreement with Muslims in this respect. And whether it is permissible to live in such a *dar harb* and obey such government's orders? In this respect, too, before a thorough discussion and quoting earlier scholars, it seems appropriate to quote a *fatwa* by the late *Mawlana* ᶜAbdul Hayy which is included in *Majmuᶜah-e fatawa* (vol. 2, p. 5):

سوال : اگر مسلم به استیمان به دار الحرب رود پس مسلم را بـه حربی در آنجا سود دادن یا گرفتن درست است یا نه ؟

جواب : نزد امام ابو حنیفه وامام محمد جائز است .

*Question:* If a Muslim enters a *dar harb* after seeking
security [permission and assurance of safety from
its authorities] then is it proper or not for the
Muslim to take or give *riba* in transactions with
*harbis* there?

*Answer:* According to *Imam* Abu Hanifah and *Imam*
Muhammad it is permissible.

He goes on to say: 'Taking *riba* from *harbis* in *Dar al-harb* is
permissible,' and quotes the following [Hanafi *fiqhi* text] as
a proof:

إذا دخل المسلم دارَ الحرب بأمان فلا بأس بـأن يـأخذ منهـم أموالهـم
بطيب أنفسهم بأي وجه كان ، لأنه إنما أخذ المباحَ على وجه عـري
عن الغدر فيكون ذلك طيبا له . والأسير والمستأمن سواء حتى لـو
باعهم درهما بدرهمين أو بـاعهم ميتـة بدراهـم أو أخـذ مـالا منهـم
بطريق القمار ، فذلك كله طيب لـه (إبن عـابدين ، رد المحتار على الـدر
المختار [للحصكفي] ، كتاب البيـوع ، بـاب الربا ، ط: دار الكتب العلمية ،
بيروت ١٩٩٤ ، ج٧، ص ٤٢٣) .

If a Muslim enters *dar al-harb* after securing *aman*
[security/assurance of safety from its authorities], there is
nothing wrong for him to take from *harbis* their property
in every possible manner with their consent. Because if he
takes what is permissible for him, without cheating, it will
be proper for him. Both the prisoner and the security-
seeker are equal in this respect[40]: it is all right even if he
sells them one *dirham* for two *dirhams*, or if he sells them
dead animal for money or takes their money through
gambling. All this is proper [lawful] for him.

---

[40] May Allah reward him the best! What a wise thing he has said!
A member of a slave community living peacefully under an
alien rule is equal to a prisoner. I would rather say that even
prisoners are sometimes in a better condition. A bird in
captivity is at least free to cry:

مجھے بھی اذنِ فغان مل سکے تو مرغِ اسیر
ترے قفس سے بدل لوں میں آشیاں اپنا

O bird in captivity! If I too were to get permission to cry,
I would exchange my nest with your cage!

171

Thus it becomes evident that according to both earlier and later *fuqaha'* there may be a kind of *dar al-harb* where Muslims may be in peace, enjoy legal rights to reside in that country and they are not bound to emigrate or go for *Jihad*, and in these conditions the security-enjoying Muslims will have the right to seek wealth through all means allowed by the government laws without consideration of whether they are prohibited under the *Shari'ah*. The only condition is that such dealings are made with non-Muslims. But, at the same time, it is not permissible for a Muslim to give *riba* to a non-Muslim because giving *riba*, in fact, amounts to giving him an opportunity to oppress Muslims. And it may be a greater sin in *Dar al-harb* — nearly as great as the sin of a soldier who gives ammunition from his magazine during fighting to a soldier of the opposing force.

In the foregoing quotation, a *musta'min* has been allowed to conclude lawful dealings according to the law of the land, but contrary to the Islamic laws, with other people only when Muslims benefit and the property of the non-Muslim is obtained with his consent, but there is no permission anywhere to give our property to them. So in such a *dar harb* where a security-enjoying Muslim is living in peace and is not forbidden from performing his religious rites but in money matters he is not governed according to Islamic law, he is permitted to take *riba* from a non-Muslim but he is not allowed to give *riba* to the non-Muslim. But if the Muslim is compelled to borrow from a non-Muslim and he fears for his life in case he does not borrow, in such a case he can borrow from a non-Muslim on *riba*. This dealing will be treated at par with the case where even carcass-eating is permissible when dying of starvation for lack of food. And those Muslims will bear the burden of this sin who, in spite of being capable, did not help their brother-in-need, or those *'ulama* who did not hold *qard hasan* as obligatory and tied the hands of wealthy Muslims by giving *fatwas* for non-permissibility of *riba* and put them in a state where the saying of *Sayyidna* 'Ali: يعضّ المؤسر على ما في يديه (the rich will clinch their fists)[41] became applicable to them.

---

[41] See above, p. 110.

# FATWA
# ON BANK INTEREST & INSURANCE

An *Istifta'* (query)[42]
about bank-interest and insurance
and its reply by the late
*Mawlana* Sayyid Ahmad ᶜAli Saᶜid
(then Grand *Mufti* of Darul ᶜUlum (Waqf), Deoband)

Respectable Grand *Mufti*, may your blessings continue!

Kindly explain [your stand on] the following questions:

(1) The issue of *sood* [usury] is common now. Amounts deposited in banks attract *sood*. Is it permissible to use the *sood* given by banks? And if the receipt of such an amount is allowed, is it allowed for the receiver to use it or not? And if it is not allowed then how should this amount be used?

(2) It is said and believed generally that there is no way one can avoid *sood*. For instance, farmers' needs are tied to the [co-op] societies for fertilizers etc, on which interest has to be paid. Loans taken for trade bear interest, etc. So is there any way-out or not within the rules of the present government?

---

[42] Translated from the text published in *Tarjaman-e Darul ᶜUlum Jadeed* (2: 8-9, (Delhi, January, February 1995). Emphasis through underlining has been added by the editor. The Arabic texts used in the two appendices have been left as they appeared in the original writings, *i.e.*, no authentication has been done by us (ed.).

(3) People say about the two-fold and three-fold amounts given against five and ten-year [deposit] schemes of banks that such amounts are profits and therefore there is no objection to them. Another excuse for accepting them is that in this way a lump sum is accumulated which would otherwise be quite impossible. Masses prefer logical and rational reasons, therefore please explain the issue in this way.

(4) These days insurance has gained currency. What is its legal position?

Kindly give a detailed reply in the light of traditional and rational reasoning so that the masses would be enlightened and would be able to lead their life according to the Islamic principles.

*Hamid Hasan Qasimi*
Servant of Madrasah Faydul ʿUlum
Siyal Nagla, Post: Habbi, Distt. Meerut, U.P.

## [*Mufti's* reply]

*The reply seeking Allah's help is as follows:*
The Question of *sood* [usury] is not new. Usury-based transaction was common even in the pre-Islamic days. It used to take the shape of extending the duration of a monetary loan against raising the amount to be paid at the end. It is said in *Fat-h al-Bari*, a commentary on *Sahih al-Bukhari*, that,

كان الربا في الجاهلية أن يكون للرجل على الرجل حق إلى أجل فإذا حلّ قال : تقضي أم تُربي . فإن قضاه أخذ وإلا زاد في حقـه وزاد الآخر في الأجل .

*Riba* in the days of *Jahiliya* [pre-Islam] was as follows: A man has lent someone a sum for a specific period and when the time for payment comes, he tells the debtor: 'will you pay or should I increase the amount?' If the debtor paid the sum the creditor took it, and if not, he raised his sum and thereby extended the duration for payment by the debtor.

*'Allamah* al-Jassas has said in his *Ahkam al-Qur'an*:

إنه معلوم أن ربا الجاهلية إنما كان قرضا مؤجلا بزيادة مشروطة فكانت الزيادة بدلا من الأجل فأبطله الله وحرمه .

It is known that the pre-Islamic *riba* was a loan for a duration extended by increasing the amount payable. The increasing of the amount was against extending the time limit for payment. Allah invalidated this and made it unlawful.

This is why Allah said:

يَمْحَقُ اللهُ الرِّبَا وَيُرْبِي الصَّدَقَاتِ (البقرة : ٢٧٦)

Allah deprives usury of all blessing, but gives increase for deeds of charity (2:276).

In another Qur'anic verse, Allah said:

أَحَلَّ اللهُ الْبَيْعَ وَحَرَّمَ الرِّبَا (البقرة : ٢٧٥)

Allah hath permitted trade and forbidden usury (2:275).

In a third verse, Allah said:

يَا أَيُّهَا الَّذِينَ آمَنُوْا لاَ تَأْكُلُوا الرِّبَا أَضْعَافاً مُّضَاعَفَةً وَّاتَّقُوا اللهَ لَعَلَّكُمْ تُفْلِحُوْنَ (آل عمران : ١٣٠) .

O ye who believe! Devour not usury, doubled and multiplied; but fear Allah; that ye may (really) prosper (3:130).

It is learnt from this that *riba* is a great sin and an injustice. Allah has made it unlawful, while *sadaqah* (charity) which is for the sake of Allah, is commendable and a cause for the increase of wealth.

In the *Jahili* system, usury-based transactions were practised both for loans and trade. The Qur'anic verses have invalidated both the usury-based trade and usury-based loans. Usama ibn Zayd has narrated that: إنما الربا في النسيئة The Prophet, upon whom be peace, said '*riba* is in credit [delayed payment] transactions.'

In another *hadith*, Abu Sa'id al-Khudari has narrated that the Prophet said:

لا تبيعوا الدرهم بالدرهمين، فإني أخاف عليكم الربا، والربا هو الربا .

175

Do not sell one *dirham* for two *dirhams* because I am afraid that you will commit *riba*. And *riba* is *riba*.

The gist of the Prophetic *hadiths* about *riba* is that it is not limited to transactions of money [coins] but includes many other forms. For instance taking two *tolas* of silver against one *tola*, or two kilograms of wheat against one kilogram is also unlawful. The *hadith* has banned all forms of *riba* from the Islamic economic system.

Now the question arises about the meaning of *riba*, or 'sood,' literally and as a terminology, which is utterly unlawful and *haram* in the light of the Holy Qur'an and *Hadith*.

*Riba* is an Arabic word which means to charge an increased amount in a monetary transaction even if such an increase is normal[ly accepted]. There is a consensus in the *Ummah* that there are two kinds of *riba*: *riba hissi* (perceptible *riba*) and *riba hukmi* (considered *riba*). The words الفضل ربا (the increase is *riba*) in the authentic *hadith* is about the perceptible *riba*. The words of a *hadith* in *Al-Bukhari* الذهب بـالذهب مثـلا بمثـل (gold for gold, quantity for quantity) is an explanation of the perceptible *riba*. And this is the definition of the transaction legally considered as *riba*. This is why it has been described as: الفضل الخالي عن العوض) an increase devoid of compensation).

The Law-giver has considered even familiarity as *riba hissi* where the transaction is not hand-to-hand. Therefore *riba* depends on late payment in which an increase is involved. This is the meaning of the *Sahih Muslim hadith* لا ربا فيما كـان يدا بيـد (there is no *riba* in a hand-to-hand transaction).

The 'considered *riba*' has been explained in the Prophet's *hadiths*: نهى النبي صلى الله عليه وسلم عن بيع دينار and الذهب بالورق ربا.

Shah Waliullah Dehlawi, may Allah's mercy be upon him, has given the following comprehensive definition of *riba*:

الربا هو القرض على أن يؤدى اليه أكثر وأفضل مما أخذ (حجة الله البالغة ، ج،
ص ١٦٢)

*Riba* is the loan [given] on the condition that it be returned with an increase and in better [quality]..

**176**

The above details show that *riba* is found in both loan and trade. Both *ribas*, whether charged by a money-lender or a trader, are unlawful. An increase, conditional or as per practice, in any obligation is *riba*.

The above inferences make it clear that taking or giving *riba* is a major sin, *haram* and unjust. But for any amount or increase in a transaction to become *riba* it is necessary that both the amounts [the original capital and the increase on it] are inviolable [legal/legally protected]. If one amount is inviolable and the increase on it, according to the Hanafi *fiqh*, is not considered inviolable but a violable [unprotected] one, then such an increase will not be considered *riba*. If someone considers it *riba* the very description will be wrong and that increase will not be considered *haram* in the light of the Qur'anic *ayahs* and *hadiths*. It is said in *Al-Bada'i wa'l-Sana'i* (vol. 5, p. 192):

وأما شرائط جريان الربا فمنها أن يكون البدلان معصومين فإن كان أحدهما غير معصوم لا يتحقق الربا عندنا (البدائع والصنائع، ج ٥، ص ١٩٢) .

The condition for the occurrence of *riba* is that both the moneys should be inviolable, and if one of them was not inviolable then *riba* will not occur in our view.

*Allamah* Shami has said (*Shami*, vol. 4, p. 244) that,

ومن شرائط الربا عصمة البدلين وكونهما مضمونين بالإتلاف وعدم تقومه لا يمنع ، فشراء الأسير أو التاجر مالَ الحربـي بجنسه متفـاضلا جائز (الشامي، ج ٤، ص ٢٤٤) .

Among the conditions of *riba* is that the two moneys should be inviolable and their destroyer could be obligated to pay compensation. There will be no *riba* if this condition does not apply. Therefore, a prisoner or a trader is allowed to buy the property of a resident of *Dar al-harb* with an increase in kind.

In addition to this, *Al-Durr al-Mukhtar* (*Shami*, vol. 4, p. 260) says:

177

ولا ربا بين متفاوضين وشريكي عنان إذا تبايعا من مال الشركة ولا
بين حربي ومسلم مستأمن بعقد فاسد أو قمار لأن ماله ثمة مباح
فيحل برضاه . وقال في رد المحتار : فلا بأس بأن يأخذ منهم أموالهم
بطيب أنفسهم بأي وجه كان، لأنه إنما أخذ المباح على وجه عري
عن الغدر فيكون ذلك طيبا له . والأسير والمستأمن سواء حتى لو
باعهم درهما بدرهمين أو أخذ مالا منهم بطريق القمار فذلك كله
طيب له (الشامي، ج ٤، ص ٢٦٠) .

There is no *riba* in the transactions of two trading partners
if they buy using the partnership money. There is no *riba*
between a resident of *Dar al-harb* and a Muslim living
there with permission even if the contract is invalid or
involves gambling because the property of the resident of
*Dar al-harb* is lawful there and its acquisition is lawful with
his consent. It is said in *Radd al-muhtar* that there is no
harm if he [a Muslim] takes their [*dar al-harb* residents']
properties with their consent because he is taking lawful
property without deceiving them, therefore it is *halal* for
him. The prisoner and a Muslim living in *Dar al-harb* with
permission are equal in this respect. It is permissible even if
he sells them one *dirham* for two or takes their money by
gambling. It is all proper for him.

It is clear from these texts that the property of a non-
Muslim in *Dar al-harb* is not inviolable for a Muslim.
Instead it is permissible to obtain it in any way whatsoever
with the consent of the *harbi* [resident of *Dar al-harb*]. The
conditions of *riba* will not apply to such a transaction and
to term it as *riba* is incorrect. Moreover, this is the view of
*Imam* Muhammad, *Imam* Sufyan al-Thawri and *Imam* Al-
Awza᷇i, may Allah's mercy be upon them.

For a Hanafite, the view of the *Imam* [Abu Hanifah],
may Allah's mercy be upon him, has preference and is
binding. And if *Imam* Muhammad also agrees with his
[Abu Hanifah's] view then it is even more powerful and
binding. It is said in *Rasm al-Mufti* (p. 72) that,

فيحل الإفتاء بقول الإمام بل يجب وإن لم نعلم من أين قـال . وعلى
هذا فما صححه في الحاوي أي من أن الاعتبار لقوة الدليل مبني على

ذلك الشرط . وقد صححوا أن الإفتاء بقول الإمام، فينتج من هـذا
أنه يجب علينا الإفتاء بقول الإمـام وإن أفتى المشـائخ بخلافـه (رسم
المفتي، ص ٧٢) .

It is not only permissible but obligatory to give *fatwa*
according to the view of the *Imam* [Abu Hanifah] even if
we do not know what his basis for saying so is. *Al-Hawi's*
assertion that the power of a proof has to be taken into
account is also dependent on this condition. Moreover,
*fuqaha'* have stipulated that the *fatwa* will be issued
according to the saying of the *Imam* [Abu Hanifah]. The
gist of the sayings of the *fuqaha'* is that the saying of the
Greatest *Imam* [Abu Hanifah] is obligatory for us even if
the *shaykhs* have given *fatwa* contrary to it.

The definition of *Dar al-harb* is that the supreme power
there should belong to a non-Muslim and his orders are
obeyed therein. It is said in *Jami' al-fusulayn*, and also in
*'Allamah* Sarakhsi's commentary on *Al-Siyar al-kabir*,
which is an important book by *Imam* Muhammad, that
there are only two kinds of *dar* (abodes): *Dar al-Islam* and
*Dar al-harb*. Then *Dar al-harb* is further divided into two
kinds: *Dar al-sharr wa'l-fasad* (abode of evil and dissension)
and *Dar al-aman* (abode of peace). As an example, he says
that Makkah before its conquest was an abode of evil. Then
came the order to migrate from it. Muslims migrated to
Abyssinia where the supreme power lay in the hands of a
non-Muslim, a Christian, who had not accepted Islam by
then. His rule was supreme there. But Muslims were given
protection of all kinds including the religious freedom. The
king gave them peace. Thus Abyssinia, although a *dar harb*,
represented the other kind of *dar al-harb*: the abode of
peace. It is said in *Majmu'ah qawa'id al-fiqh* (p. 288) that,

دار الحرب هو خلاف دار الإسلام يعني ما غلب فيهـا غـير المسـلمين
وبإجراء أحكام أهل الشرك (ص ٢٨٨) .

*Dar al-harb*, contrary to *Dar al-Islam*, is the place where
non Muslims hold sway and enforce the rules of the people
of polytheism.

179

Likewise Islamic laws are not enforced in India. People of polytheism hold sway. The supreme power is in the hands of non-Muslims. This is why India is undoubtedly a *dar harb*. But the constitution of the secular government has given security and religious freedom to Muslims so that they can act according to their religion. This is why this country is called *Dar al-amn* (abode of peace). The right to vote or a Muslim's holding high posts or being a minister has nothing to do with his being a Muslim. Moreover, all these high functionaries are subject to the supreme power and the country's constitution. Therefore, there [is no logic in] some people questioning how could this be a *dar harb* if [Muslims] enjoy the right to vote and participate in government. Even if their view point is conceded to an extent, it is clear that this country is a *Dar al-harb* because Islamic laws are not enforced and supreme power, prime ministership and presidency are in [the hands of] non-Muslims. The above Arabic text shows undoubtedly that this country is a *dar harb*. Likewise Russia, China, America, Britain and France etc, where Muslims enjoy security, are *Dar al-harb* according to the definition of the *fuqaha'*. Muslims in these countries have the status of a security-seeker (*musta'min*). This is why, according to the *Sharh Siyar Kabir*, the second category of *Dar al-harb* is called *Dar al-amn* (abode of security). And taking two *dirhams* against one in *Dar al-harb*, according to the views of *Imam* Abu Hanifah and *Imam* Muhammad is valid because the definition of *riba* does not apply to the extra *dirham* taken. Hence it is not *riba*.

Likewise the amount deposited in a bank and the extra amount paid by the bank on that deposit is not *riba* according to *Imam* Abu Hanifah and *Imam* Ahmad. The second [reason] is that the amount deposited is not a loan so that the dictum of كل قرض جر نفعا فهو ربا (every loan extracting a profit is *riba*) could be applied to it. It is well-known that the bank trades. So anyone depositing money in the bank will be considered a partner in the bank's trading in proportion to his deposit, making this a form of *mudarabah*. In this way, not considering the extra amount as *riba* and thereby rescuing Muslim economy from ruin is itself a religious need. Harming Muslim economy and society by branding this extra amount as *riba* is against religion and a proof of one's lack of intelligence and wisdom. It is said in *Al-Shami* (vol. 4, p. 245) that 'not all invalid transactions are *riba*' إن البيوع الفاسدة ليست كلها من الربا (ج ٤، ص ٢٤٥). But this rule will not be applicable where the supreme power belongs to Muslims. And it is not correct to term as *Dar al-harb* a country where [Islamic] punishments are not enforced and [yet] there is a Muslim government. In such a country the above-mentioned rules will not be held valid.

(2) It is utterly *haram* and illegal to take or give what is considered *riba* according to the Hanafi *maslak*. But for severe needs, for trade or any other necessary need, there is allowance for taking loans in accordance with the rule laid down by the *fuqaha'* that 'necessities permit the prohibited' (الضرورات تبيح المحظورات). This will be applicable if no money is available without *riba*. But it will also be necessary that there should be no laxity in paying back such a loan. Every effort should be made for earliest repayment so that one is saved from paying multiplied *riba*.

(3) For a reply to this question, please refer to reply no. 1 above. A non-Muslim organization, be it a bank or otherwise, gives two-fold or three-fold amounts with its pleasure and without any excuse. According to the Hanafi *maslak* of Imam Abu Hanifah to call this amount as interest or *riba* is an irrelevant expression.

(4) *Bima* (insurance) is not an innovation of the present age or the British period. It started in 1400 CE in some European countries like Italy, Armenia and Holland etc. And the reason for this was that if traders' goods sent to other cities or countries by boats and ships got sunk or looted by pirates, they faced bankruptcy and their trade folded up. Since every trader was a potential victim, therefore they resolved to solve this problem by paying collectively a monthly or an annual sum to

181

any trader whose goods were sunk or looted by pirates. They started acting upon this resolution until this tradition came to Turkey via Andalus in around 1480 CE during the reign of Sultan Muhammad Fateh. Thereafter it was adopted in Syria and Egypt also. It became popular in India, too, with some variations.

*Bima* is called *Sawkarah*[43] سوكرة in Arabic and 'insurance' in English, which means assurance. It is said that the insurance company assures the seeker of insurance that it will indemnify him for his losses and protect him against unforeseen threats. This is why such a company is called 'insurance company.'

The amount that the company charges in the name of insurance is loaned to others and interest is charged from the debtors, or the company benefits from this money by buying property or doing business with it. The insurance company earns enormous amounts of money as profits or interest without spending its own money and the company pays to the insured the determined excess money according to its laws.

According to our information, the company assures that its aim is to help people in difficulties and distress and the aim of the insured is to ensure that his money is safe and that it grows and the money finally received helps his children and others in need. And if an accident takes place unexpectedly and a harm takes place the insurance company will make good the loss.

The sentiments of the helper are commendable because even the Qur'an has appreciated the sentiment of cooperation for the good, and the Prophet's *hadith* has described its virtues. The aim of the seeker of insurance for the above purpose is not against the Islamic ideology. The Prophet, upon whom be peace, has said:

إنك أن تدع ورثتك أغنياء خير من أن تدعهم عالة يتكففون الناس.

For you to leave your inheritors without need is better than leaving them dependent begging from others.

---

[43] The current Arabic term for insurance is *ta'min* تأمين (ed.).

182

The insurance current in India takes a number of forms, *e.g.*: (1) life insurance, (2) car, shop or company insurance, *i.e.*, insurance of things owned by someone (3) insurance for marriage of daughters and education of children etc.

In previous times there was no life or marriage or education insurance. In early times commercial merchandise transported by ships was insured. Then goods transported by surface were also insured. *Ulama* in Syria and Egypt were divided on this. One group saw it [insurance of surface goods] valid, the other saw it as invalid. All these *ʿulama* were residents of Muslim countries. The insurers were Muslims and non-Muslims alike. In other words, the insurance companies were owned by Muslims as well as non-Muslims. In India many new forms have been introduced like the insurance of properties, life, hand, foot, brain, education and the like.

Two issues require investigation. The first is: whether the excess amount paid by the company in the name of 'dividend' is *riba* in the *sharʿi* sense or not? The second issue is the amount paid if the insured died prematurely or his property like shop or factory is destroyed or damaged by fire or by any other factor, and the amount payable after the expiry of the appointed date, or if the insured stops paying his premiums, his previously paid premiums are endangered. Does this transaction for these considerations not fall under gambling. These are the two main issues regarding insurance: *riba* and gambling and the *sharʿi* ruling in this case.

As far as the first issue is concerned, that is whether the excess amount given is *riba* or not, or if it is help and assistance, it would be stated according to the Hanafi *maslak*, to which the Hanafis are obligated, that it does not seem proper to describe this profit as *riba*. We have explained this in our reply to question 1. For further explanation we cite the instance of Al-ʿAbbas, may Allah be pleased with him. According to the *Sharh* of the *Siyar Kabir*, al-ʿAbbas had sought the permission of the Prophet to live in Makkah after he embraced Islam. The Prophet, upon whom be peace, granted him this permission. ʿAbbas continued to engage in *riba* business in Makkah until its conquest, despite the fact that the verse 'Devour not usury, doubled and multiplied' (3:130) had been revealed at the time of Uhud. Makkah was conquered about eight years later. And when Makkah was conquered the Prophet did not invalidate Abbas' previous *riba* transactions. This is because prior to its conquest, Makkah was a *dar harb*. But those transactions were annulled where *riba* was yet to be paid and the amounts of *riba* were yet to be received (*Sharh Siyar Kabir*, 2/162).

It is known from this that the profit taken from a *harbi* [resident of *Dar al-harb*] is not *riba*, provided it is not derived through deception and without such a person's consent.

*Fuqaha'* have allowed *'uqud fasidah* [invalid contracts] in *Dar al-harb*. Although *fiqhi* works have stipulated this only for a *musta'min*[44], but an authoritative book like *Siyar Kabir* has also allowed a *harbi* Muslim[45] to do such business:

ثم قد علم أن الربا لا تجري بين مسلم وحربي في دار الحرب (شرح السير الكبير، ج ٣، ص ١١٢) .

It is known that *riba* does not occur between a Muslim and a *harbi* in *Dar al-harb* (*Sharh Siyar Kabir*, 3/112).

As regards invalid contracts, it is not only *Imam* Abu Hanifah who says it, even *Imam* Malik believes that it is permitted. But in his [*Imam* Malik's] *mad-hab*, the stipulation is that there should be no peace [treaty] between *Dar al-harb* and *Dar al-Islam*. It is said in the *Mudawwana al-kubra*:

سئل الإمام مـالك : هل بين المسلم (إذا دخـل دار الحرب) وبين الحربي ربا ؟ فقال الإمام : هل بينكم وبينهم صلح ؟ قالوا : لا، فقال مالك لا بأس في ذلك (المدونة الكبرى، ج ٢، ص ٢٨١) .

---

[44] '*Musta'min*' مستأمن is a person who enters *Dar al-harb* after securing '*aman*' أمان, *i.e.*, promise of security and safety, from its authorities. It is like the current practise of securing entry visas before entering foreign countries (ed.).

[45] '*Harbi* Muslim' is a Muslim normally living in *Dar al-harb* (ed.).

*Imam* Malik was asked: Is there *riba* between a Muslim (if he enters *Dar al-harb*) and a *harbi*? He said: is there peace between you and them? They said: no. In which case, Malik said, there is no harm in it (*Al-Mudawwanah al-kubra* p. 281).

It is clear that there is no *Dar al-Islam* in the vicinity. There are Muslim states on two sides but they are not *Dar al-Islam* because Islamic laws and punishments are not enforced there. Even [Muslim] personal laws are not properly enforced here [India]. Even the insurance companies belong to non-Muslims. Thus whatever excess amount they offer at their pleasure, even if they call it 'interest,' it is not *riba*. Just by calling it *riba*, a permitted money or amount does not become *riba*.

Now the second issue: is there gambling in this? Abu Bakr al-Jassas has said under the [exegesis] of the verse about gambling:

ولا خلاف بين أهل العلم في تحريم القمار، وأن المخاطرة من القمار.
قال ابن عباس : إن المخاطرة قمار وإن أهل الجاهلية كانوا يخـاطرون
على المال والزوجة وقد كان ذلك مباحا إلى أن ورد تحريمه.

There is no difference among the people of knowledge about the unlawfulness of gambling and that taking risk is gambling. Ibn ᶜAbbas has said that taking risk is gambling and that people in the *Jahiliyah* [pre-Islamic period] used to take risk about money and wives. It was allowed until its unlawfulness was announced by revelation.

The summary of this is that taking risk about one's money and being in the dark about the result is *qimar* (gambling). Thus a dealing where there is money from both sides and the result is not known is gambling whether it takes the shape of buying and selling or insurance. And the unlawfulness of gambling is proved by the revealed text.

In reply to question number one, we had quoted the following text from *al-Shami* (vol. 3):

بخلاف المستأمن في دار الحرب فإن له أخذ مالهم برضاهم ولو بربا
أو قمار لأن مالهم مباح لنا إلا أن الغدر حرام (الشامي، ج ٣، ص
٣٤٥).

With the exception of a *musta'min* in *Dar al-harb* who is
allowed to take their moneys with their consent even if it is
through *riba* or gambling because it is permissible for us to
take their moneys but treachery is not allowed.

This shows permissibility of taking moneys from a non-
Muslim in *Dar al-harb* through gambling. But this is not all;
there should be a further condition that [the Muslim] must
have the expertise that there should be no danger of him
losing his money; instead, he must be sure of winning. It is
not allowed at all if there is a danger of losing one's money.

*Allamah* Zayn al-*Abidin*, in his book, *Al-Shami*, has
mentioned *sawkarah* (insurance) three times. In the chapter
on *'musta'min'* he has dealt with it in detail. This could be
taken as his *fatwa* since he says at one point: وبما قررناه يظهر
جواب ما كثر السؤال عنه في زماننا (what we have clarified is a reply
to what is an oft-repeated question in our time).

The following are the last lines of his writing on this subject:
ولا يخفى أن صاحب السوكرة لا يقصد تغرير التجار ولا يعلم
بحصول الغرق هل يكون أم لا ؟ وأما الخطر من اللصوص والقطّاع
فهو معلوم له وللتجار لأنهم لا يعطون مال السوكرة إلا عند شدة
الخوف طمعا في أخذ بدل الهالك . فلم تكن مسئلتنا من هذا القبيل
أيضا . نعم ! قد يكون للتاجر شريك حربي في دار الحرب فيعقد
شريكه هذا العقد مع صاحب السوكرة في بلادهم ويأخذ منه بدل
الهالك ويرسله إلى التاجر . فالظاهر أن هذا يحل للتاجر أخذه لأن
العقد الفاسد جرى بين حربيين في دار الحرب وقد وصل إليه مالهم
برضاهم فلا مانع من أخذه . وقد يكون التاجر في بلادهم فيعقد
معهم العقد هناك ويقبض البدل في بلادنا لا يقضى للتاجر بالبدل وإن لم
يحصل خصام ودفع له البدل وكيله المستأمن هنا يحل له أخذه لأن
العقد الذي صدر في بلادهم لا حكم له فيكون قد أخذ مال الحربي

**186**

برضاه . وأما في صورة العكس بأن كان العقد في بلادنا والقبض في
بلادهم فالظاهر أنه لا يحل أخذه ولو برضا الحربي لابتنائه على العقد
الفاسد الصادر في بلاد الإسلام فيعتبر حكمه (الشامي، ج ٣، ص
.(٣٤٦)

It is obvious that the intent of the insurer is not to deceive
traders, nor does he know if [the ship] will drown or not.
As regards the danger from robbers and waylayers, he as
well as the traders know it because they do not pay the
insurance money except due to the severity of fear, in the
hope of getting [compensation] in lieu of the lost goods.
The issue at hand is not this. The [Muslim] trader might
have a *harbi* partner in *Dar al-harb;* this partner concludes
the agreement with the insurer in his country and takes
the compensation for the lost property and sends it to the
trader. It is obvious that the trader is allowed to take this
because the invalid contract has taken place between two
*harbis* in *Dar al-harb* and their money reaches him with
their consent; therefore there is no objection to his taking
this money. It may also happen that the [Muslim] trader is
in their country; he concludes the contract there and takes
possession of the compensation in our country, there will
be no verdict in the trader's favour [in *Dar al-Islam*] even if
there is no dispute [but] if his *musta'min* agent pays him
the compensation, he will be allowed to take it because the
contract having been concluded in their country has no
validity. In this case it will be construed that he takes their
money with their consent. But if the opposite happens,
that is that the contract is concluded in our country and
the payment of [compensation] is made in theirs, it is
obvious that he is not allowed to take it even with the
consent of the *harbi* because it is based on an invalid
contract effected in the lands of Islam and, therefore, its
[legal] position will be subject to [the laws of] Islam (*Al-Shami*, 3/346).

It is clear that an invalid contract has no place in Islam but it
is legal in *Dar al-harb*. Likewise if a non-Muslim's money is
taken in *Dar al-harb* with his consent, it is not *riba;* instead
it is receipt of a permissible money:

187

وما أخذ برضاهم ليس غدرا من المستأمن، بخلاف المستأمن منهــم في
دارنا لأن دارنا محل إجراء الأحكام الشرعية فلا يحــل لمسلم في دارنا
(الشامي، ج ٣، ص ٣٤٥) .

What is taken with their consent is not deceit on the part
of the [Muslim] *musta'min*. But it is [deceit] in the case of a
*musta'min* from them [*dar al-harb* residents] in our land
because our land is where *shar'i* rules are applied; therefore
it is not allowed for a Muslim in our land (*Al-Shami*,
3/345).

It is clear from this that the rules about contracts and
dealings are different in accordance with the abode [*dar al-
Islam* or *dar al-harb*]. There was no *riba*-based insurance in
the time of *'Allamah* Shami, or it could not happen in the
Muslim State of that time, therefore his *fatwa* does not
mention *riba*. But he mentions the change of rules in
respect of invalid contracts in *Dar al-Islam* and *Dar al-harb*
with illustrations of both. We have referred to them in
brief.

It is valid to accept according to the *maslak* of the *Imam*
[Abu Hanifah] and Imam Muhammad, may Allah's mercy
be on them both, that the excess money received from a
bank or an insurance company is not *riba*. Change of name
will not change the reality:

قد علم أن الربا لا يجري بين المسلم والحربي في دار الحرب (شرح السـير
الكبير، ج ٣، ص ١١٢) .

It is known that *riba* does not occur between a Muslim and
a *harbi* in *Dar al-harb* (*Sharh Siyar kabir*, 3/112).

There is gambling in insurance and gambling is unlawful
and prohibited. From this point of view insurance loses its
permissibility. Any dealing where there is money on both
sides and the result is not known while the danger [of losing
one's money] is strong, will be considered gambling. There
is [this] danger in insurance. But in the present conditions
when the devil of communalism, partisanship and casteism
is dancing, innumerable riots and unilateral actions have
endangered life and property, judiciary's position is not

188

respected, places of worship have no sanctity, in such conditions, Muslims living in *Dar al-harb* will have to take into consideration the *shar'i* parallels to protect their life and property. The Noble Prophet, upon whom be peace, has said,

من قتل دفاعا عن نفسه فهو شهيد ومن قتل دفاعـا عـن عرضـه فهـو شهيد ومن قتل دفاعا عن ماله فهو شهيد .

whoever is killed defending his life is a martyr, whosoever is killed defending his honour, is a martyr, whosoever is killed defending his property is a martyr.

From this we know that the protection of life, honour and property is imperative in every condition. If one is killed defending them, he attains the high status of a martyr.

Moreover, the Noble Prophet, upon whom be peace, said in the Last *Hajj* sermon[46] that:

إن دماءكم وأموالكم وأعراضكم عليكم حـرام إلى أن تلقـوا ربكـم كحرمة يومكم هذا وكحرمة شهركم هذا.

Your lives, properties and honour are inviolable until you meet your Lord, like the sanctity of this day and this month.[47]

It is said in the book, *Al-Ashbah wa'l-naza'ir* that :

الضرورات تبيح المحظورات ومن ثَمَّ جـاز أكـل الميتـة عنـد المخمصـة وإساغة اللقمة بالخمر والتلفظ بكلمة الكفـر للإكراه وكـذا إتـلاف المال وأخذ مال الممتنـع مـن أداء الدين بغير إذنه (الأشباه، ج ١، ص .(١٤٠)

Necessities make unlawful lawful. Therefore, it is lawful to eat dead meat in hunger, to make the food palatable with wine or to utter words of unbelief due to coercion. Likewise, it is permissible to destroy property and to take

---

46  See full text in Zafarul-Islam Khan (ed.), *Al-Hajj: hikmah wa rumuz* (London 1985) pp. 87-90.

47  Fighting is prohibited, except for self-defence, in four *Hijri* months which include the Month of Pilgrimage *(Dhu al-Hijjah)* in which the Prophet *(pbuh)* delivered this sermon. The other three months are: *Muharram, Rajab* and *Dhu al-Qi'dah* (ed.).

possession of the property of a [solvent] person without his permission if he is refusing to pay debt (*Al-Ashbah*, 1/140).

Moreover it is said in *al-Hamawi* that,

فالضرورة بلوغه حدّا إن لم يتناول الممنوع هلك أو قارب وهنا يبيح تناول الحرام (الحموي، ص ١٤٠).

Necessity means reaching a stage where one will die or be close to death if he did not consume the unlawful. At this stage it is permissible to consume the unlawful (*Al-Hamawi*, p. 140).

It is perhaps for this reason that in 1964 the Council of Shar⁽i Research, Lucknow, the Jam⁽iyatul ⁽Ulama and the *muftis* of Darul ⁽Ulum, Deoband, allowed the insurance of life etc in view of the present conditions of India. It is said in the *Hadith* that لا تجتمع أمتي على ضلالة (my *Ummah* will not unite on falsehood). Therefore, it is in the best interest of the Muslims to consider the above mentioned verdicts of the ⁽ulama and *muftis* as the correct verdict for the present time. It is a religious necessity that life and property be saved. Moreover, it is a step towards the betterment of the economic and social conditions of the Muslims.

It is not correct to say that this will lead to the evaporation of the belief in the unlawfulness of *riba* and gambling from the minds of the Muslims. The *riba* which is unlawful will remain unlawful in every condition. But it is the obligation of the ⁽ulama and *muftis* to clarify the issue. It is said in the fundamental books of *fatwas* that in this age the responsibility of the *mufti* is only to copy. They are copiers, not *mujtahids* [makers of independent judgements]. *Fiqhi* works clearly state the stand of the *Imam* [Abu Hanifah] and *Imam* Muhammad, may peace be on them both. But this has not been publicized and Muslims have not been informed about them. It was necessary to teach Muslims that both taking and giving *riba* is unlawful. But at the same time it was necessary to tell the Muslims that at the place where you live now, if you give a non-Muslim one *rupee* and take back two *rupees*, it will not be *riba* at all. The result of this non-clarification was that the Muslim could not profit; instead, he paid usury and by paying usury upon usury sacrificed his properties, houses, lands and orchards.

When the British rule started in India after the fall of the Muslim state, this matter should have been clarified. But the British were apprehensive that if India is dubbed as '*dar al-harb*,' Muslims will be hell-bent on fighting [the British rulers]. Although this notion of theirs was wrong, the British tried hard that India is not declared '*dar al-harb*'. And the *ulama* due to their compulsions and fear for their life and property could not clarify this matter. As a result this matter remained unsolved among the neglected dossiers [of the Muslim community].

It is clear from pondering over the writings of the *fuqaha'* that India is a *dar harb*. We have clarified this in our reply to question number one. It may be added here that a great scholar of India and the *Shaikh al-Hadith* of Darul ʿUlum, Deoband, ʿAllamah Sayyid Muhammad Anwar Shah Kashmiri, may Allah's peace be upon him, has written:

بهر حال تسلّط کفار بر هند بدان درجه است که در هیچ وقت کفار را بر دار الحرب زیاده نه بود، وادائے مراسم اسلام از مسلمانان محض باجازت ایشان است، واز مسلمانان عاجز ترین رعایا کسے نیست

The supremacy of the non-Muslims over India is such that such supremacy has never been seen before in any *dar harb*. Whatever rituals of Islam Muslims can undertake is by their permission [like the permission according to the clauses 25, 26 of the Indian constitution]. There is no community more powerless than Muslims here.

Shah Sahib has written this about the British period. But there is no doubt about India being a *dar harb* in the light of the conditions and the bases for a country's being a *dar harb* or a *dar Islam* as described by him. He has said that,

بايد دانست كه مدار بودن بلده يا ملك دار الاسلام يـا دار الحـرب
بر غلبه مسلمان وكفار است وبس

Let it be known that for determining a city or a country to
be a *dar Islam* or a *dar harb*, the supremacy of Muslims or
non-Muslims is sufficient.

After this clear-cut clarification we are constrained to say
that India is a *dar harb* and it is correct without doubt to
give a non-Muslim one *rupee* and take back two *rupees* from
him with his consent because this [excess amount] is not
*riba*.

# Rethinking the 'riba' issue

Excerpts from an article[48]
by *Mawlana* Muhammad Zafiruddin,
*Mufti*, Darul ʿUlum, Deoband

I can now understand that, what *Mawlana* Sayyid Manazir Ahsan Geelani, the former head of the Department of Theology, Jamia Osmania [Hyderabad] wrote during the British period about لا ربا بين المسلم والحربي فى دار الحرب (there is no *riba* between a Muslim and a *harbi* in *Dar al-harb*) was correct. It is based on the *mursal*[49] narrative of Mak-hul مكحول which has been accepted by the Greatest *Imam* Abu Hanifah and *Imam* Muhammad and there is no doubt that the *mursal* narrative of a trustworthy narrator is acceptable in principle.

If we accept the *Mawlana*'s opinion even in these times, a lot of the problems of the Muslims in this country will be solved and the scope of this point of view will be widened.

I once had a discussion on this issue with the *Mawlana*, upon whom be Allah's peace. He said that in this country we have to deal with the non-Muslim day and night. They believe that it is valid for them to take *riba* from us and

---

[48] Excerpts on *riba* from *Mawlana* Zafiruddin's article, 'Kiya mawjuda dawr mein beema karaaney ki ijaazat hai?,' *Tarjaman Darul ʿUlum Jadeed*, 2:5 (Delhi, October 1994) pp. 29-35. Here the section on insurance has been ignored since it is almost identical to the earlier *fatwa* reproduced in appendix one above. Emphasis through underlining has been added by us (ed.).

[49] *Mursal* مُرسَل ('hanging') is a *hadith* narrated by a narrator who has not personally met the person he is narrating from (ed.)

they take it. In this one-way trade a lot of the Muslim wealth has been transferred to them through this channel. Muslims are left poor and bankrupt. We issued the *fatwa* that *riba* is unlawful, so Muslims could not take it [*riba*] from non-Muslims. There are thousands of opinions narrated on the authority of the *Imams* Abu Hanifah and Muhammad and we abide by them and do not care about what the three [other] *Imams* [Malik, Shafi'i and Ibn Hanbal] say about such issues. We bring forth our arguments to give preference to such opinions over the opinions of the [other] three *Imams*.

Now when we say let us act according to the opinions of *Imam* Abu Hanifah and *Imam* Muhammad on this issue [*riba*], the ᶜ*ulama* start sermonizing but no one addresses the premises put forward in our articles. You may have read those articles which appeared in the *Maᶜarif* magazine at the time and in which objections were answered. But our ᶜ*ulama* of Deoband did not issue their *fatwa* in its favour out of caution. Now the country is free, times have changed and we do not know what kind of situations may arise in future. What happened in Hyderabad[50] is in front of our eyes. You people will have to use deep thinking and far-sightedness.

During the discussion, *Mawlana* Geelani also said that you should keep in view the issue of slavery. Is it not an insult to humanity? But the Noble Prophet, upon whom be peace, validated it because the opponents used to treat us as such and used to make us slaves and slave-girls. Despite this the Mercy to the World [Prophet], upon whom be peace, specified the rights of the slaves and slave-girls, gave orders with special emphasis to treat them properly, exhorted

---

[50] During the so-called 'police action' against the princely State of Hyderabad (Deccan) in September 1949, the Indian army committed massacres against Muslims. An estimated 200,000 persons were allegedly killed by the army and supporting armed groups, in addition to large-scale destruction of property, confiscation of properties and lands and large-scale expulsion of Muslims from jobs. Even today nothing is known about many victims who disappeared during the Indian invasion (ed.).

Muslims to free them and explained the recompense for this act. He did this so that slaves are not considered sub-human or subjected to treatment injurious to their humanity. It is correct that there were other interests and reasons.

What I would like to submit is that even this issue presents a way for the validation of insurance, while it solves many other problems. Therefore, there is no harm in thinking over this formula.

We should make use of the facilities Islam has given in *Dar al-harb* and *dar al-kufr*. Today Hanafi scholars, seeking facilities are ready to ignore many opinions of the Hanafi *madh-hab* and are publishing long articles about it. What hell will be let loose if we act according to the opinion of *Imam* Hanifah and *Imam* Muhammad and ignore the opinions of the three *Imams* and *Imam* Yusuf?

Where ʿAllamah Shami has treated the issue of *sawkarah*, which is a form close to insurance, he has expressed his inclination towards its unlawfulness in *Dar al-Islam* but at the same time he has said that there is no harm in it in *dar al-harb*:

بخلاف المستأمن في دار الحرب فإن له أخذ مالهم برضاهم ولو بربا أو قمار لأن مالهم مباح لنا إلا أن الغدر حرام . وما أُخِذ برضاهم ليس غدرا من المستأمن، بخلاف المستأمن منهم في دارنا لأن دارنا محل إجراء الأحكام الشرعية (رد المحتار) .

With the exception of a *mustaʾmin* in *Dar al-harb* who is allowed to take their money with their consent even if it is through *riba* or gambling because it is permissible for us to take their money but treachery is not allowed. Whatever is taken with their consent is not treachery on the part of the *mustaʾmin*. On the contrary, a *mustaʾmin* from them in our lands [is not allowed this] because ours is a land where *sharʿi* rules are applied.

Let us think about the basis on which a *mustaʾmin* is allowed [to take 'riba' in *dar al-harb*]. Does this basis obtain in this country or not? If it does, let us think seriously and decide with broad-mindedness.

# LIST OF SOURCES
### used to authenticate the Arabic texts in the book

القرآن الكريم.

البدائع والصنائع للكاساني ، القاهرة ، ١٣٢٨ / ١٩١٠.

التفسير الكبير للرازي ، دار الكتب العلمية ، بيروت ، ١٩٩٠.

احج حكمة ورموز لظفرالإسلام خان (تحقيق)، المعهد الإسلامي، لندن، ١٩٨٥.

حجة الله البالغة للإمام ولي الله الدهلوي ، القاهرة ، دارالتراث ، ١٩٧٧.

رد المحتار [لإبن عابدين] على الدر المختار [للحصكفي] ، ط: دار الكتب العلمية، بيروت ١٩٩٤.

سنن أبي داؤد ، دار إحياء التراث العربي ، بيروت ، ب.ت. / اسطنبول ١٩٩٢.

سنن ابن ماجة ، ط: دار إحياء التارث العربي ، بيروت / أسطنبول ١٩٩٢.

سنن الترمذي بشرح ابن العربي، ط. دار إحياء التراث العربي، بيروت ، ب.ت.

سنن الدارقطني ، دارالكتب العلمية ، بيروت ، ١٩٩٦.

سنن الدارمي ، القاهرة ، دار الفكر ، ١٩٧٨ / دارالكتب العلمية ، بيروت ١٩٩٦.

شرح معاني الآثار لأبي جعفر الطحاوي ، ط: دار الكتب العلمية ، بيروت ، ١٩٩٦.

صحيح البخاري مع فتح الباري، ط:دار إحياء التراث العربي، بيروت ، ١٤٠٢.

صحيح البخاري، ط : ١، المطبعة السلفية ومكتبتها ، القاهرة ١٤٠٣هـ.

صحيح النسائي ، ط: دار الكتب العلمية، بيروت ، ، ب.ت.

صحيح مسلم ، ط. ٢ : اسطنبول ، ١٩٩٢.

فتاوى قاضيخان (على حاشية الفتاوى العالمكيرية ، بولاق ، ١٣١٠ هـ / ١٨٩٢.

القاموس المحيط للفيروزابادي الشيرازي ، دار الكتب العلمية ، بيروت ، ١٩٩٥.

كتاب السير الكبير للشيباني ، حيدرآباد الدكن ، ١٣٣٥هـ / ١٩١٦.

مؤطأ الإمام مالك ، ط: ٢ ، بيروت : دارالنفائس، ١٩٧٧.

المبسوط للسرخسي ،، بيروت ١٤٠٦ هـ / ١٩٨٦.

مسند أحمد بن حنبل ، دار سحنون ودار الدعوة ، استنبول ، ١٩٩٢.

معالم التنزيل للبغوي (مطبوع مع تفسير الخازن)، ط. دار الكتب العلمية، بيروت ١٩٩٥.

الهداية للمرغيناني، ط: كتب خانه رشيدية ، دهلي ، ب.ت.

*The Holy Bible* (the Authorised (King James) Version), The Gideons International, n.p., 1976.

**196**

# GLOSSARY

*ᶜalim* عالم = scholar

*ahadith* أحاديث = pl. of *hadith* (q.v.)

*Ahl al-Sunnah* أهل السنة = Sunni school of jurisprudence (*fiqh*)

*bayᶜ* بيع = trade, sale, transaction.

*bayᶜ sarf* بيع صرف = exchange of coins and currencies (*sarrafah*)

*bayᶜ muratalah* بيع مراطلة = barter

*bayᶜ salaf* بيع سلف = advance sale / purchase, credit dealing

*dar al-harb* دار الحرب = 'enemy territory', *i.e.,* non-Muslim territory

*dar al-Islam* دار الإسلام = territory of Islam, *i.e.,* where Islamic laws are enforced

*faqih* فقيه = learned in *fiqh* (q.v.).

*fatwa* فتوى = legal opinion given by a scholar or *mufti* (q.v.).

*fiqh* فقه = Islamic jurisprudence

*fuqaha'* فقهاء = plural of *faqih* (q.v.)

*Hadith* الحديث = corpus of the narrations about the sayings and deeds of the Prophet *(pbuh)*

*hadith* حديث = a saying of the Prophet *(pbuh)*

*haram* حرام = forbidden, illegal, unlawful.

*harbi* حربي = resident of *dar al-harb* (q.v.)

*imam* إمام = leader of the Muslim community, great scholar, leader of congregational prayers.

*istifta'* استفتاء = query of juristic/legal nature put to a *mufti* (q.v.).

*khutbah* خطبة = sermon, lecture

*madh-hab* مذهب = school of Islamic jurisprudence

*maslak* مسلك = sub-school of Islamic jurisprudence/ thought.

197

*mufti* مفتٍ = established scholar in Islamic laws who can, or is authorised, to issue *fatwa (q.v.)*

*muhaddith* محدّث = compiler or narrator of *ahadith*, like Al-Bukhari and Muslim.

*muhaddithun* محدثون = plural of *muhaddith (q.v.)*

*muratalah* مراطلة = barter trade.

*musta'min* مستأمن = seeker of *aman* أمان (security/safety), a person who enters enemy or foreign territory with permission from that territory's rulers, like a person securing entry/residence visa these days to go to a country or reside there.

*mustahabb* مستحب = commendable (but not obligatory) deed

*nasi'ah* نسينة = credit, deferred payment

*pubh* = peace be upon him, صلى الله عليه وسلم : the Islamic salutation to the Prophet whenever his name is mentioned.

*qard hasan* قرض حسن = 'good loan,' *i.e.*, soft loan without collateral which the debtor has to return when and if he is able to do so.

*riba al-fadl* ربا الفضل = *riba* in hand-to-hand dealings.

*riba al-nasi'ah* ربا النسينة = *riba* in credit dealings.

*ruku*ᶜ ركوع = one section of the Qur'an.

*sadaqah* صدقة = voluntary charity

*sahaba* صحابة = plural of *sahabi (q.v.)*

*sahabi* صحابي = companion (of the Prophet)

*sarf* صرف = exchange

ᶜ*ulama* علماء = plural of ᶜ*alim (q.v.)*

*wajib* واجب = obligatory

*Zakat* زكاة = obligatory charity [for the rich]